THE
INTERPERSONAL
COMMUNICATION
SKILLS WORKSHOP

THE INTERPERSONAL COMMUNICATION SKILLS WORKSHOP

Listening • Assertiveness
Conflict Resolution • Collaboration
A Trainer's Guide

Joshua D. Guilar

AMACOM

American Management Association

New York • Atlanta • Boston • Chicago • Kansas City • San Francisco • Washington, D. C.
Brussels • Mexico City • Tokyo • Toronto

Special discounts on bulk quantities of AMACOM books are available to corporations, professional associations, and other organizations. For details, contact Special Sales Department, AMACOM, a division of American Management Association, 1601 Broadway, New York, NY 10019.
Tel.: 212-903-8316. Fax: 212-903-8083.
Web site: www.amacombooks.org

This publication is designed to provide accurate and authoritative information in regard to the subject matter covered. It is sold with the understanding that the publisher is not engaged in rendering legal, accounting, or other professional service. If legal advice or other expert assistance is required, the services of a competent professional person should be sought.

Library of Congress Cataloging-in-Publication Data

Guilar, Joshua.
    The interpersonal communication skills workshop : Listening, Assertiveness, Conflict Resolution, Collaboration
        p.   cm
    Includes bibliographic information and index.
    ISBN 0-8144-7085-8
    1. Interpersonal communication. 2. Interpersonal relations. 3. Group relations training.
I. Title.

HM1166.G85 2001
302.2—dc21   00-063994

Printing number

10 9 8 7 6 5 4 3 2 1

CONTENTS

   Materials   148

   Checklist   148

   Overhead 4-1. Conversations for Coordinating Action   148

   Scope and Sequence   148

Lecture Notes: Conversations for Coordinating Action   149

   Introduction   149

      Exercise 4-1. Gauging the Commitment of Participants   149

      Overhead 4-2. Three Questions   149

      Overhead 4-3. Module Agenda   150

      Overhead 4-4. Module Agenda (Cont.)   150

      Overhead 4-5. Module Objectives   150

   Personal Commitments   150

      Overhead 4-6. Your History of Commitments   151

      Workbook Activity 4-1. Your History of Commitments   152

      Workbook Activity 4-2. Your Work Commitments   154

      Overhead 4-7. Projects and Commitments   156

   Overhead 4-8. What Is It Time For?   156

   Preview: Five Conversations for Coordinating Action   157

      Workbook Activity 4-3. Ranking Your Commitments   158

      Overhead 4-9. Five Conversations for Coordinating Action   159

   Conversations for Connection and Relationship   159

      Overhead 4-10. Conversations for Connection   160

      Overhead 4-11. Listening For . . .   160

      Overhead 4-12. Authenticity   161

      Overhead 4-13. Authenticity (Cont.)   161

      Overhead 4-14. Emotional Intelligence   161

      Overhead 4-15. Seeing Each Person as Unique   162

   Conversations for Cocreation   163

      Overhead 4-16. Interpersonal Creativity   164

      Overhead 4-17. Interpersonal Creativity (Cont.)   164

      Overhead 4-18. ?Fi Tahw   165

      Overhead 4-19. What If?   165

      Overhead 4-20. Living What If   165

      Overhead 4-21. Living What If (Cont.)   165

      Exercise 4-2. The What If Exercise   165

ACKNOWLEDGMENTS

Many people contributed to making this book possible, particularly my teachers in many institutions throughout the years—Oregon State University, the Portland Apprenticeship Committee, the University of Oregon, and Hewlett Packard.

I would like to thank the people at Suffolk University who now make my life more productive, particularly the Chair of the Department of Communication and Journalism at Suffolk University, Bob Rosenthal, who suggested that I write this book.

My colleagues at AMACOM, Jacquie Flynn and Christina McLaughlin, provided much wisdom and expertise for improving this book.

My son, Nate Guilar, is a great supporter in all my aspirations in life.

Last but not least, I would like to thank all the trainees and students who have worked with me over the years. You have made my career possible.

I thank the international students who study in the United States for bringing your cultures to us. And I thank the students in Belarus and in Senegal who give me the opportunity to work in such fascinating countries.

CONTACT INFORMATION

For twenty-five years Joshua Guilar has worked in training and development. His expertise is the delivery and development of instruction. He is a professor in the Department of Communication and Journalism at Suffolk University in Boston.

He invites you to contact him regarding feedback for this book and regarding his work as a consultant in training and development.

Joshua Guilar
Department of Communication and Journalism
Suffolk University
Boston, MA 02114
Phone: 617 573-8767
FAX: 617 742-6982
jguilar@acad.suffolk.edu

PART I

WORKSHOP FRAMEWORK

Introduction

Imagine. You enter a corporate training room in the early morning. Participants are seated at tables around the room. You feel enthusiastic as you come in because you are prepared and ready to go. The room is properly set up for your training session. Everything is in place. You know the participants will engage skills and knowledge that can change their lives forever.

Welcome to *The Interpersonal Communication Skills Workshop.* This guide provides you with what you need to prepare and deliver an outstanding two-day workshop in interpersonal communication.

American businesses invest as much as $30 billion a year on training and development in communication. Success in business often depends on effective communication among coworkers, clients, and partners. This book explains how to train people as communicators in order to meet the demands of the twenty-first century.

Although the need for training in communication is recognized, not all such training is effective. Unfortunately, some training is ill conceived and some trainers are ill prepared. This book is the antidote. The result of the author's twenty-five-year career in communication training, this guide is based on sound and proven principles.

The book features leading-edge trends in interpersonal communication training, including:

1. Applications of adult learning theory unique to interpersonal communication training

2. Task-by-task processes for training

3. Performance orientation

4. Proven methods such as accelerated learning and action learning

5. Focus on communication skills for collaboration and organizational learning

This introduction gives an overview of the workshop, explaining how to use this book and how to become an excellent workshop trainer.

OVERVIEW OF THE TRAINER'S GUIDE

This guide has three parts. In this first part, the introduction to the material, you have what you need to set up the workshop. Topics include the agenda and pre-work, marketing, and project management.

The heart of the book is part 2, which contains four workshop modules. Each module is four hours long. These can be taught all together as a two-day workshop or individually as four-hour modules. The four modules are:

1. Powerful listening

2. Assertiveness

3. Conflict management

4. Conversations for coordinating action

The four modules cover interpersonal competencies required to be an effective collaborator in organizations. The first module, "Powerful Listening," provides an introduction to the workshop and exercises for learning to listen and to connect powerfully with others.

"Assertiveness," the second module, details techniques for building support for ideas. The module also explains the PRES model for advocacy as well as exercises for expressiveness.

"Conflict Management," the third module, enables workshop participants to understand the nature of conflict and to analyze and resolve conflicts effectively. The final module, "Conversations for Coordinating Action," explores how to get things done collaboratively. Trainees learn how to establish accountability through making clear requests, promises, and declarations.

This trainer's guide provides extensive materials for teaching these topics. Each module has the following sections:

- Introduction
- Instructional plan
- Content and example presentations
- Overheads
- Workbook activities
- Instructions for flipchart designs

- Teaching tips
- References to resources

Your job is to study these materials, customize them as desired, and use them to conduct the workshop.

Part 3 of the book provides resources for evaluation and preparation. "Evaluation and Follow-up" covers what to do to assess, improve, learn from, celebrate, and communicate the value of the workshop. "Resources for Trainers" contains a reading list as well as websites, associations, networks, and other sources for the interpersonal communication trainer. There is also a segment on career development for trainers.

Now that you have an overview of the workshop and the book, let us turn to a step-by-step process for setting up the workshop. A successful workshop does not stand alone. Activities carried out before and after the workshop help integrate the workshop into the lives of participants.

WORKSHOP PREPARATION

In his book *Smart Training,* Clay Carr questions the practice of training for its own sake. According to Carr, training should serve to improve people's performances.[1] To do this, you need to help people change their everyday behavior, which is no small task. Even if you present sound principles and model useful skills in the workshop, there is no guarantee that the participants will use these skills when they return to the workplace. Put another way, there is no guarantee of the *transfer of learning.*

Improving the transfer of learning requires careful preparation before the workshop and thorough follow-up afterward. This section explains what to do before the session. Here is a preview of topics:

- Getting your ducks in a row
- Budget
- Marketing communication
- Assessment of learners
- Transfer of learning
- Facilities
- Instructional preparation
- Project management

GETTING YOUR DUCKS IN A ROW

Great training does not occur by accident. Whether you are an internal trainer employed by an organization or an external trainer hired by a client organization, the same principles apply. Training takes planning and the efforts of many. Here is a list of the people with whom you need to build relationships.

- *Training managers.* What are their needs and interests? What advice can they give? What other resources can they provide?
- *Organization management.* The more connected you are with management, the more leverage you have in the organization. What are the managers' interests and needs?
- *Trainees.* What are the needs and aspirations of trainees?
- *Other trainers and consultants.* Your success in training depends on your network of resources. Who else could you involve in helping this organization? What might they know that could be useful?

Getting your ducks in a row means getting to know this organization and connecting with your partners. Your success depends on working within the organization's unique culture. Be sensitive to culture. Obtain as many materials as possible—even recruitment or public relations brochures. Orientation materials given to new employees are helpful. Ask your clients as much as possible about their organization's history, present, and vision for the future.

Be aware of potential land mines or sensitivities. Here is an example:

> Bob was a trainer with great materials who failed to be sensitive to the nature of the organization he was working with. He gave a leadership seminar in a closely held corporation. One person owned this large, profitable manufacturing organization. Unfortunately, some of Bob's motivational examples were about stock options and profit sharing—neither of which was available in this company. People began to resent Bob's examples, which made him less successful.

Customize your examples and materials to fit the culture. Keep the managers apprised of what you are doing. The work of partnership building never ends. Develop networks based on mutual interest.

BUDGET

You and your client have a number of costs associated with this workshop. Be aware of these costs, and make sure you know both your wants and needs and those of your client. Costs include:

- Cost of managing—both your training business and theirs
- Costs of workshop development—including any preparation and customization you have to do as well as printing materials and ordering supplies
- Costs of facilities—food and, in the event of a residential setting, housing
- Indirect costs for participants—their time, travel, preparation, and follow-up
- Your costs—travel, housing, and meals
- Equipment costs—provision and maintenance of projectors, VCRs, and screens
- Promotional materials—mailings and advertisements
- Unanticipated costs—additional travel, follow up, and supplies

FIGURE I.1

WORKSHOP ADVERTISEMENT

INTERPERSONAL COMMUNICATION WORKSHOP

Powerful skills for relational intelligence and breakthrough performance

Date: Time:

Place:

Topics: **Benefits:**

- Powerful listening

- Assertiveness

- Conflict management

- Conversations for coordinating
  action

This workshop is for all levels of
employees.

- Attain powerful listening as a basis
  for connection and mutuality.

- Improve performance through
  establishing effective networks for
  action.

- Learn tools for authenticity, self-
  confidence, influence, and advocacy.

- Gain competencies for
  productive negotiation and
  conflict management.

Instructor:

Contact:

Your contract with your client should cover all costs associated with the workshop and who pays for what. Also, pay attention to the return on investment. Given all the costs, how does the training affect the performance of the organization?

MARKETING COMMUNICATION

The workshop begins for each participant the first time he or she hears about it. The advance messages help shape participants' attitudes toward you and the workshop. Carefully craft your key messages and their timing. Figure I.1

shows an example of a promotional flyer for the workshop. Note that the spaces for date, time, place, instructor, and contact person are empty. Complete these as appropriate.

You will have to customize your advertising for each unique event. In some cases, internal training staff will handle this step through e-mail. Make sure to get across key information such as logistics, topics, and benefits to participants.

ASSESSMENT OF LEARNERS

At the heart of adult learning is the participant—the adult who has needs, experience, and aspirations. These workshop materials target professionals and managers working in today's organizations. However, you must customize this training to a specific group of people. The more you know about the needs of the adults you teach, the better trainer you will be.

Here are some ways you can use information about your participants. You can:

- Emphasize and expand on the communication skills these specific people need in their work situations.

- De-emphasize or delete content that might not work for their needs and organizational culture.

- Find examples related to their situation. For example, employees of a corporation that is being taken over by another company can benefit from stories about interpersonal relationships in other such situations.

- Take into consideration the backgrounds of participants. Participants might already have advanced skills in communication. If so, teach advanced content. If not, emphasize the basics.

- Include trainees' specific requests. If you survey participants before the training, you can incorporate their strengths, weaknesses, and objectives into your material.

- Involve participants in the training before it begins. By establishing contact with trainees early (even in written form), you begin integrating the training into their everyday lives.

Figure I.2 is a sample of a survey you can send to participants prior to the workshop. Be sure to check with internal partners, such as training managers, to ensure that the survey is appropriate.

In filling out the survey, participants think about their development in communication. Conversations with trainees before and after the workshop aid in the transfer of learning.

TRANSFER OF LEARNING

Failure to ensure transfer of learning might be the major cause of ineffective training.[2] Researchers Broad and Newstrom have found that as much as 80 percent of training can be ineffective because participants do not use the skills

FIGURE 1.2

WORKSHOP PRE-SURVEY

INTERPERSONAL COMMUNICATION WORKSHOP PRE-SURVEY

Introduction:

You are enrolled in the Interpersonal Communication Workshop. In this workshop, you will gain skills to improve your effectiveness and collaboration. By completing the pre-survey, you will help the workshop facilitator to customize instruction to your needs.

Name, position, and a brief description of what you do:

_____
_____
_____

Your strengths as a communicator:

_____
_____
_____

Your greatest challenges as a communicator:

_____
_____
_____

Please rate your competence from one to five in the following communication areas.

	Weak				**Strong**
Listening	1	2	3	4	5
Assertiveness	1	2	3	4	5
Conflict Management	1	2	3	4	5
Coordinating with Others	1	2	3	4	5

What do you want to accomplish in the upcoming workshop?

_____
_____
_____

Thank you for completing the survey.

FIGURE 1.3

PROBLEMS AND SOLUTIONS FOR TRAINERS CONCERNING TRANSFER OF LEARNING

Problem	Solution
• Trainer does not plan for transfer of learning.	• Co-plan for transfer of learning with key partners—trainees, managers, human resources, and training department.
• Trainer does not include transfer of learning in instruction.	• Include transfer of learning in the instruction by applying it to real-life situations. • Give homework at the end of each session. • Ask participants what they will take from the session and apply in their work.
• Trainer does not fully engage learners in the content.	• Model the competencies. • Engage learners in focused objectives.

taught when they are back on the job.[3] Helping trainees employ these skills in their everyday work is essential. If they do not use them, they lose them. Your investment and theirs are wasted!

Ensuring the transfer of learning is about helping people make changes. Learning is defined as a change in behavior and influencing these changes is the core of your success as a trainer.

There are three potential forces working against the transfer of learning. First, the trainees themselves might not make the connection between the content of the training and their work. Second, the trainees' management might work against the behaviors learned by the trainee. Finally, organizational systems and culture might also work against the new behaviors.

Transfer of learning begins with the trainer responsible for the instructional system. Figure I.3 shows problems and solutions for trainers seeking to help participants transfer learning. The trainer needs to involve *everyone*—the trainees, their managers, human resources, and the training department—in planning how to transfer learning. Also, the trainer needs to give homework and ask participants questions that help them take what they learn back to their work.

Figure I.4 shows the ways trainees can be involved in the transfer of learning. These processes begin with trainees giving input into workshop content with the workshop pre-survey (see figure I.2). Also, you can ask trainees to

FIGURE I.4

PROBLEMS AND SOLUTIONS FOR TRAINEES CONCERNING TRANSFER OF LEARNING

Problem	**Solution**
• Trainees do not see workshop skills as important.	• Involve participants in determining workshop content using the pre-workshop survey and other methods.
• Trainees do not connect workshop content with their work projects.	• Assess training needs related to work projects prior to workshop using the pre-workshop survey and other methods. • Include action learning projects in the workshop—trainees work on their actual work projects during the session.
• Trainees forget content, get distracted, and do not follow up with the skills and knowledge.	• Build follow-up activities, such as development plan reviews, mentors, and support groups or partners. • Provide a participant workbook or job aids that provide easy access to methods.

work during the session on projects from their jobs—identifying a particular project that involves a network of people, for example. Finally, participants can use techniques to continue to develop skills after the workshop ends. Examples are getting mentors, organizing support groups, putting together development plans, and using the participant's workbook as an ongoing reference and job aid.

Participants' managers also play a role in the transfer of learning, as shown in figure I.5. Train managers first so they know and use the skills participants will learn. Involve managers in customizing workshop content with an instrument similar to the workshop pre-survey or through focus groups. Involve managers in activities after the workshop such as development plans and mentor programs. Most important, managers can follow up on the development of skills in the everyday work of participants.

The final level is the organizational system (see figure I.6). What exists in the organizational system that could reinforce training? One example is mutual reinforcement between the workshop and organization development interventions. Look for synergy with human resources (HR) practices such as development

FIGURE I.5

PROBLEMS AND SOLUTIONS FOR MANAGERS CONCERNING TRANSFER OF LEARNING

Problem

- Managers do not support skills learned by participants.

Solution

- Pretrain managers.
- Involve managers in customizing the workshop content.
- Communicate with managers before and after the workshop.
- Involve managers in follow-up activities, such as development plans, mentors, and support groups or partners.
- Integrate content of training in the everyday supervisory process.

FIGURE I.6

PROBLEMS AND SOLUTIONS FOR ORGANIZATIONS CONCERNING TRANSFER OF LEARNING

Problem

- The organization does not give ongoing reinforcement.

Solution

- Tie in with organizational development interventions.
- Involve the organization—management, human resources, and the training department.
- Reinforce with organizational policies such as development plans.
- Connect with business plans and strategies.

plans and recruitment (e.g., recruit people whose experience fits with these skills). Finally, figure out how the workshop orientation—communication competence—fits with the business plan and strategy of the organization.

Planning for transfer of learning can be crucial to the effectiveness of the workshop. Another area for planning regards the workshop facilities.

FACILITIES

Where will the workshop be held—in an on-site training room or a residential setting? Often, organizational constraints will make the choice for you. A residential setting has advantages for learning interpersonal communication. You want participants to get past their ordinary reactions and everyday thinking. You also want them to have time for reflection, time away from interruptions such as voice mail and e-mail. A residential setting also gives members of a work or project team an opportunity to bond with each other.

Whatever the facility, it needs to be accessible, large enough for the participants, and furnished with comfortable chairs and tables for writing. Carefully consider the space. The workshop itself is a conversation in which listening and speaking is ongoing for all, and physical space affects the nature of this conversation.

Figure I.7 gives three possible seating arrangements. Drawing A shows a U-shape, with the instructor at the front. This arrangement encourages interaction among participants. However, trainees sitting on the same side have a difficult time seeing each other. Drawing B shows a number of circular tables distributed throughout the room. Seating participants at tables dispersed around the room encourages interaction between them, which is desirable. Because many of the exercises involve pairs, seat an even number of participants at each table. Drawing C shows row seating, which accommodates a larger number of participants and does not provide tables for writing. If you use this design, form the chairs into a curve so participants can see each other better. Because there are no tables for writing, be sure that the participants' workbooks are stiff enough to write on easily.

Also, figure I.7 shows the arrangement of flip charts and the overhead or computer display. You also need a table to hold handouts and other materials. Consider such details as food and refreshments, location of bathrooms, and storage space for coats and so forth.

INSTRUCTIONAL PREPARATION

You have the option of customizing the instructional materials. Using the materials in this book and your analysis of the organization and the participants, consider making the following changes.

- Add, delete, expand, or de-emphasize content areas.
- Find relevant examples and stories to support your major points.
- Make notes of these changes.

FIGURE I.7

ROOM CONFIGURATIONS

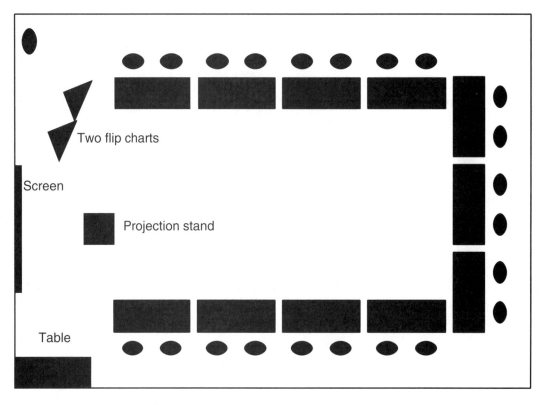

Drawing A. U-shaped room.

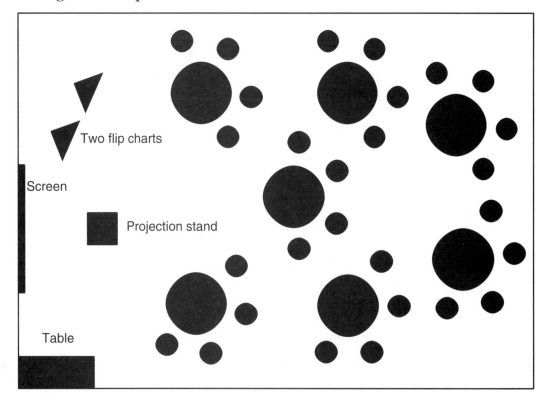

Drawing B. Circular tables.

FIGURE I.7 (CONTiNUEd)

ROOM CONFIGURATIONS

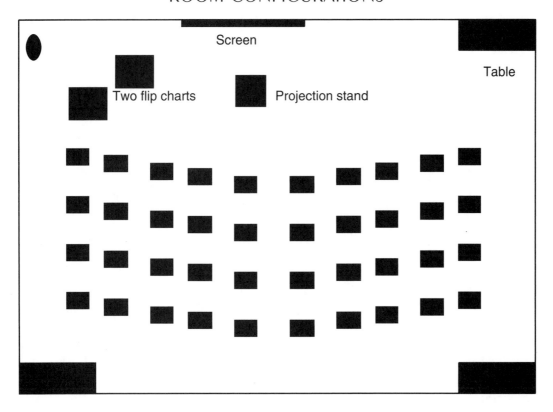

Drawing C. Row seating.

- Make copies of overheads or computer display files as appropriate.
- Finish and assemble participant handbooks.
- Prepare flip-chart pages in advance.
- Determine measures to assess the effectiveness of the workshop.

Participant workbooks are not furnished with this trainer's guide. However, all the resources to create one are available. Each module contains workbook activities, which are compiled sequentially in appendix B. Participants can use these handouts for activities. You can also easily expand these materials into a workbook for each trainee by adding a title page, copies of the overheads (see appendix A), and additional blank pages for writing their thoughts and notes. A note of caution: Only include the negotiation worksheet for workbook activity 3.1. Do not include the case study pages, because the parties in that particular role-play should not have access to each other's case studies. The times given in the workshop modules are approximate. Actual times will vary with the instructor and the group. Prepare contingency plans to adjust your timing. For example, you might find participants love to talk and that exercises

FIGURE I.8

ORGANIZING PRODUCTION TASKS.

	Task	Owner	Week 1	Week 2	Week 3	Week 4	Week 5	Week 6
1	Research company	Trainer	•					
2	Schedule facility	Coordinator	•					
3	Market class	Coordinator	•					
4	Enroll participants	Coordinator		•				
5	Pre-survey	Trainer		•				
6	Customize instruction	Trainer			•			
7	Determine measures	Trainer/Manager			•			
8	Review edits	Manager			•			
9	Practice instruction	Trainer				•		
10	Set up facility	Coordinator					•	
11	Prepare materials	Coordinator					•	
12	Deliver instruction	Trainer					•	
13	Administer measures	Coordinator					•	
14	Debrief	Trainer					•	
15	Follow up	Trainer						•

and discussion take longer than you thought. Have a plan for how to shorten some activities so you can finish on time and still complete the objectives.

You will also need to plan for the possibility that exercises go faster than anticipated. Work out an additional activity. Bear in mind that it is better to end early rather than late. Do not keep participants later than the agreed-upon time.

PROJECT MANAGEMENT

A workshop is a project. You will probably have partners who will share the work with you. Your aim is to provide everyone—participants and partners—with a seamless experience of your work. Take responsibility. Plan. The French have a saying, "gouverner c'est prévoir," that means "to govern is to foresee." You want to anticipate all the tasks that will make the workshop successful.

Figure I.8 shows a chart for organizing the production tasks for the workshop. The chart lists the tasks, the persons responsible (the trainer and other partners such as training coordinators and manager), and the number of weeks prior to the workshop the tasks should be completed. You can customize the chart to fit your plans and follow-up activities.

Careful planning and preparation will make your workshop successful. Getting all your ducks in a row will give you a sense of confidence about serving your clients well.

TEACHING MODULES INDIVIDUALLY OR AS A TWO-DAY WORKSHOP

The Interpersonal Communication Workshop can be taught as a two-day workshop, or it can be taught as four separate four-hour modules. Both of these strategies have benefits. If you teach the two-day workshop, then participants have the opportunity to leave their everyday concerns and concentrate on new skills for two days. You have more opportunity as an instructor and mentor to influence them. They have more time for reflection on their current reality and on changes they want to make. This experience of renewal and change can be further enhanced in a residential setting—for example, a conference center located in a natural setting.

Teaching the workshops as separate modules also has advantages. With this strategy, people need to attend for only four hours, and they are then free to take care of business for the rest of the day. This training is fast and convenient. Also, the participants might need development in the competencies of one module and not the others. They can choose which module to attend.

Teaching the modules in sequence over a period of time is another strategy. For example, hold the workshop one half day per week for a month. The benefit of this approach is long-term study and follow-up. The possible downside is a dilution of the experience and even a loss of participants over time due to attrition. If you use this strategy, ask for a firm commitment from participants to attend all four sessions.

SUMMARY

"Much good work is lost for lack of a little more."

—*E. H. Harriman*[4]

This book is a trainer's guide for the preparation, delivery, and evaluation of a workshop in interpersonal communication. The guide is a road map with resources for you to deliver world-class training.

This book provides you with the resources you need. The other element for success is internal—your hard work and preparation—so that you can deliver on your promise.

NOTES

1. C. Carr, *Smart Training* (New York: McGraw-Hill, 1992).
2. R. S. Caffarella, *Planning Programs for Adult Learners* (San Francisco: Jossey-Bass, 1994).
3. M. L. Broad & J. M. Newstrom, *Transfer of Training* (Reading, MA: Addison Wesley, 1992).
4. D. Carnegie, *Public Speaking and Influencing Men in Business.* (New York: Association Press, 1951), p. 166.

PART II

WORKSHOP MODULES

Powerful Listening

INTRODUCTION

Listening is the foundation of interpersonal communication. In this module, you will guide the participants through the information and experiences that will help improve the way they listen. By transforming how they listen to others, you can help them improve their relationships and their effectiveness. Also, you can help them become more fulfilled in their professional and personal lives.

INSTRUCTOR PREPARATION

To instruct others in listening, you must be a good listener yourself. Moreover, the quality of listening in the training room is a lesson in itself. How able are the participants to listen to one another? How well do the participants listen to you?

As the instructor, you must commit yourself to ongoing development of your listening skills. Take as much time as possible to prepare yourself. The activities outlined in this book for workshop participants are appropriate for preparing yourself. Here is a list of recommendations:

- Study the resources for trainers given in chapter 6 of this book. Join the International Listening Association listed there.

- Familiarize yourself with the history of training and development in listening and with listening research.

- Speak with others who have taught or taken courses on listening to find out what did and did not work.
- Keep a journal of your listening experiences and observations.
- Practice the skills explained in this book aimed at improving listening.
- Become aware of your strengths and weaknesses as a listener.
- Create a personal plan for development in listening.

As a trainer, you are a model and a coach for others as they develop their listening skills. Know your limits. How well prepared are you to teach listening? How many courses in listening have you taught? What level of personnel did you teach? Answer these questions, and prepare yourself accordingly.

✓ Materials

Assemble these materials before the session.

- ❏ Overhead transparencies or slide show for Module 1 and appropriate equipment
- ❏ Two flip-chart pads on easels and markers
- ❏ Flip-chart pages prepared with content and titles
- ❏ Participant workbooks
- ❏ Trainer's workshop guide
- ❏ Folding paper cards (tents) for participants to write their names
- ❏ A talking stick for exercise 1-3; (this is optional and can be any object you like)

✓ Checklist

Check the facility carefully before the participants arrive.
- ❏ Does the equipment work?
- ❏ Are tables and chairs arranged appropriately?
- ❏ Are windows, doors, and lighting comfortable?
- ❏ If the break includes refreshments, are they set up?
- ❏ Do you know the location of rest rooms and telephones?
- ❏ Do you know the numbers and contacts for emergency assistance?
- ❏ Are the flip charts set up with markers?
- ❏ Are name tents available with markers?

Facilitator: Display overhead 1.1 as participants arrive. Full-size overheads appear in appendix A.

> **Interpersonal Communication Workshop**
>
> Powerful skills for relational intelligence and breakthrough performance
>
> _____
>
> 1.1   © 2001 Joshua D. Guilar

Scope and Sequence

This chapter begins with an introduction to the two-day workshop and to module 1. The session itself covers the competencies in the model for powerful listening—volition, attending, understanding, memory, responding, and development. The section on each feature within the model contains a brief theoretical perspective followed immediately by application. Powerful listening is the foundation for effective interpersonal communication in organizations and for the Interpersonal Communication Workshop.

LECTURE NOTES: INTRODUCTION

Total time: **4 hours**
Midpoint break: **15 minutes**
Time for segment: **30 minutes**

Prepare your introduction carefully to make a positive first impression. In the introduction you want to accomplish the following:

- Introduce yourself in a positive and appropriately personal way.
- Establish your credibility for this topic and group.
- Make sure the participants are comfortable with one another.
- Produce an atmosphere conducive to listening, learning, and sharing.
- Create identification with the participants—for example, determine your common interests.
- Define the topic, agenda, and objectives clearly.
- Engage the learners in the workshop.

Customize these objectives to fit yourself and the group.

The following is an example introduction. Examples of instructor comments appear throughout the book. Again, tailor the introduction to your situation.

> Good morning. I am [your name], and I am excited to be with you at [name of organization]. For more than [mention number of] years, I have worked with organizations to help people develop skills in interpersonal communication. I would like to begin with introductions. In this workshop we will spend time communicating, so it is appropriate that we get to know each other. I'll begin.

Training Tip: Introducing Yourself

Remember that as an instructor you are an authority figure, and people need to trust you. Say positive things about yourself. If you have significant professional experience, be sure to weave this fact into your comments. You might want to mention your origins and whether you are married and have children. Also use a brief personal story about communication or a good story featuring the communication of an influential person you know in the organization.

Participant Introductions

Instruct participants to put their names on their name tents. Then ask them to introduce themselves.

> Let's go around the room. I will ask each one of you to tell us: your name; a little about your work; something personal, such as something about your family or a hobby that you have; and finally, what you would like to accomplish in this workshop. Listen carefully to each person as he or she speaks. Each moment of this workshop is an opportunity to refine our communication skills.

 Facilitator: Prepare a flip-chart page.

As you explain what you want each person to include in his or her introduction, display a flip-chart page. On it repeat the verbal instructions you gave the participants.

Introduce yourself:
- Your name
- Your work
- Something personal
- Goal of workshop

 ### Training Tip: Your Listening Skills

Demonstrate your listening skills. Give each person your whole attention, appreciation, encouragement, and thanks. Remember what the participants say. If you want, you can take notes, but if you do, make sure you still maintain good eye contact with each person. Respond appreciatively, and do not take attention away from the speaker with your comments.

Most important, memorize and use people's names. Ask for clarification as to how names are pronounced and memorize the pronunciations. Write pronunciations out phonetically if it helps.

Alternate option. Do not use the flip chart. Ask people to remember the four items you would like them to share, writing them down if necessary. Explain that remembering is a critical skill for listeners.

Suggest that participants memorize each other's names.

> I have a request. This morning's session is on listening, and it is important that we pay attention every moment. I want each of us to pay attention and to remember what each person says. If you need help remembering, I would suggest you take notes. Each of you has a participant's workbook. There are blank pages at the back. It usually helps long-term memory to take notes.
>
> Everybody set? Now, let's go around the room beginning with [name of first person you select].

Workshop Agenda

Introduce the agenda and objectives for the workshop. Begin by telling the participants the length of the workshop and its agenda. Keep to this schedule.

 Facilitator: Show overhead 1.2. Read or paraphrase each point when showing the overheads.

Workshop Agenda

- Day 1
  - *Morning session:* Powerful listening
  - *Afternoon session:* Assertiveness
- Day 2
  - *Morning session:* Conflict management
  - *Afternoon session:* Conversations for coordinating action

1.2

At this point, tell participants where the rest rooms and telephones are located. Mention any specific requests you might have, such as starting on time at the beginning of sessions and after breaks. You can also ask people to inform you if they need to be absent for any portion of the workshop.

Alternate option. State your guidelines about communication in the class. Example guidelines are listening, participation, authenticity, confidentiality, and respect for each individual. Because this session is on listening, you can easily ask participants to give their full attention to one another and to speak one at a time.

Workshop Objectives

Introduce the workshop objectives. Begin by emphasizing the workshop's importance and then state each objective.

> In our busy lives it is difficult to find the time to reflect, to learn new skills, and to work on our personal development in communication. For most of us, a workshop like this one is a rare and important

opportunity. Our purpose is to increase our effectiveness by achieving breakthrough performance as communicators.

 Facilitator: Show and explain overhead 1.3, which shows a pyramid model of the objectives for the workshop. Point out the interrelated nature of the workshop sessions.

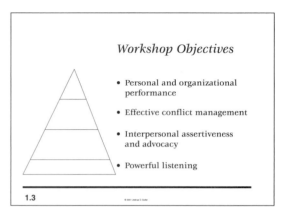

Listening comes first and forms a foundation. The connected relationships and partnerships created through powerful listening enable effective action. Listening is the basis for effective expression and assertiveness at the second level of the model. Listening also forms the basis for negotiation and for preserving the relationships that could be threatened through defensiveness on the third level of the model, or conflict management. The first three levels—listening, assertiveness, and conflict management—enable the topmost level. The top level is personal and organizational performance, which is the topic of module 4, "Conversations for Coordinating Action."

LECTURE NOTES: POWERFUL LISTENING
Introduction
Time for segment: 5 minutes

 Facilitator: Display overheads 1.4 and 1.5.

Introduce the agenda and objectives for this session. Also, let the participants know the time of the break.

Module Agenda

Total time: Four hours
- Introduction
- Element 1. Volition
- Element 2. Attending
- Element 3. Understanding

1.4

Facilitator: Show and read overhead 1.6.

The purpose of the session is for you to develop the features of powerful listening required to build those relationships, partnerships, and alliances necessary to work effectively in your organization.

 Facilitator: Display overhead 1.7.

The session objectives appear on overhead 1.7. The module's objective is to develop competence and skill with the six elements in the powerful listening model.

The overhead shows the interrelated features of powerful listening. We will be following this model throughout the session. The first element is volition. *Volition* is our willingness to listen to other people. Without wanting to listen, we cannot fulfill our potential as listeners. The second feature is *attending,* or how well we pay attention to others. The third is *understanding* other people's point of view. The fourth feature is *remembering* what people communicate, and the fifth is *responding* to people.

The graphic also shows the sixth element, or *development.* Competence in development consists of monitoring the outcomes of listening, reflecting on our practice, and improving over time. Together, the features of the model represent development of competence in listening.

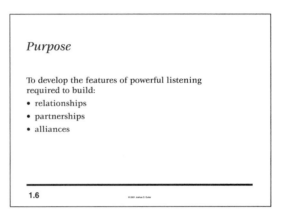

Module Agenda (Cont.)

• Break: Fifteen minutes
• Element 4. Memory
• Element 5. Responding
• Element 6. Development
• Conclusion

1.5

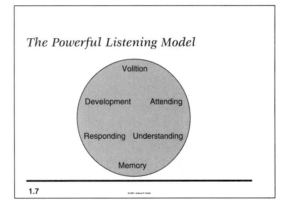

Purpose

To develop the features of powerful listening required to build:
• relationships
• partnerships
• alliances

1.6

Element 1. Volition

Time for segment: 35 minutes

Your goal in this section is to help the participants gain the will to listen, which is the basis of element 1, volition.

> Becoming a great listener is not automatic. Hearing is automatic, listening is not. Hearing is primarily a physical act involving our eardrums. Listening, in contrast, is primarily a mental process involving meaning. People often listen poorly. Paul Tournier, a Swiss psychiatrist, wrote: "It is impossible to overemphasize the immense need humans have to be really listened to, to be taken seriously, to be understood. Listen to all the conversations in our world between nations as well as those between couples. They are for the most part dialogues of the deaf."[1]
>
> The first element in the powerful listening cycle is volition, the willingness to listen. Our objective is to gain the motivation to be great listeners and to practice listening intentionally.

 Facilitator: Display overhead 1.8.

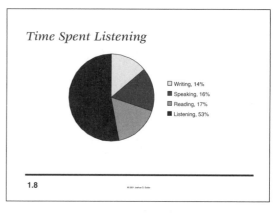

Time Spent Listening

☐ Writing, 14%
■ Speaking, 16%
☐ Reading, 17%
■ Listening, 53%

1.8

We often take listening for granted. This overhead summarizes research on communication. Adults spend about 70 percent of their waking time communicating. Of this time, they spend about 14 percent writing, 16 percent speaking, and 17 percent reading. The remaining 53 percent of their time is spent listening—21 percent in face-to-face encounters and 32 percent in electronic or mass listening.[2]

Although we spend an enormous amount of time listening, we rarely are taught *how* to listen. We spend the least amount of our actual communication time writing, but it receives the most attention in our education. Listening, the communication mode we use the most, gets the least instruction—if any.

But massive research supports the greater importance of listening for professional success in our dynamic workplace. In his influential book *In Search of Excellence,* Tom Peters states that "the excellent companies are not only better on service, quality, reliability, and finding a niche. They are better listeners."[3] In his later book *Thriving on Chaos* Peters devotes three sections to listening.

In fact, many research studies have found listening is positively related to good health as well as to career success across professions from management to law to medicine.

Chinese character for listening

 Facilitator: Put up overhead 1.9.

When reviewing the Chinese character for listening, point out that listening varies by culture and by gender. For instance, people of Asian backgrounds as well as females have been observed as being better listeners.[4] Point out the elements of the character from the lower left clockwise to the lower right.

On the lower left is the character for the word *king.* The sage king, according to Confucius, is the ultimate king. As a benevolent force in the nation, the sage king inspires people. The sage king is in contrast to the conqueror king.

The larger symbol at the upper left means the ear. The king has a large ear.

Now we move to the right-hand side of the character. The entire right-hand side means *virtue.* Confucianism centers on virtue. The top symbol refers to the eyes. We listen not only through our ears, but also with our eyes. The line in the middle means one, and the symbol at the lower right means heart.

This amazing symbol represents listening as the quality of a leader who listens with the ears, eyes, and heart in one with the self, others, and the community. Listening then is a key characteristic of leaders anywhere in an organization.

Exercise 1.1. Talk about Yourself

By now you have done a lot of speaking, so you want to move to an exercise where the participants interact.

We have taken a good look at the importance of listening, but the sorry fact is that many of us do not listen well at work or in our personal lives. When was the last time you did a poor job of listening? Also, when was the last time someone did not listen to you?

 Facilitator: Prepare a flip chart with "Why we don't listen" written at the top.

Ask the participants, "Why don't we listen?" using a flip chart. Note their responses on the flip chart. Express appreciation for and elucidate their views.

Ask for stories where appropriate. Summarize their responses. Here are some reasons why people do not listen. Add to the chart some of these reasons that the participants don't mention.

- Not interested
- Bored by others
- Too busy
- Unimpressed or uncaring
- Convinced many people are not worth listening to
- Distracted
- Preoccupied
- Thinking about what to say next
- Overloaded with information
- Thinking faster than people talk
- Confused or find the message too complex
- Daydreaming about the Caribbean
- Already know the information
- Waiting to talk about yourself

Using the last item on the list, transition to the "Talk about Yourself" exercise. In this exercise we learn that we often care more about what we want to say than about the other person's wishes.

Alternate option. You can first model "Talk about Yourself" by asking a participant to join you at the front of the room. Pick someone you like and you believe is not very defensive. Explain to the person that this exercise is a role play about how *not* to listen, so it should not be taken too seriously.

Ask the person to think about something he or she is interested in, such as a hobby or a business idea, and then to tell you about it. After he or she talks for a short while, interrupt. Talk about yourself or a related idea. If you can be humorous, this is even better. Then tell the person and the class that you were only playing the role of a poor listener. You were just demonstrating "Talk about Yourself."

Ask the same person to speak again but on a different topic. Only this time help him or her speak by using your listening and confirming skills. Then thank the participant and ask him or her, "Did you notice the difference?" Ask the class, too.

 Facilitator: Next, set up the "Talk about Yourself" exercise.

1. Form the class into pairs.
2. Explain that first you want them to demonstrate a lack of listening skills. Each pair identifies the partner who will speak first. The first

speaker talks about anything he or she is interested in. The listener will upstage the speaker. Give them only one and a half minutes to talk.

3. Switch roles, letting the listener speak and the speaker listen.

4. Debrief the exercise. Ask the participants, "What was that like?" Usually, they will say it was awful but familiar.

The second time around is the reverse of "Talk about Yourself."

1. Ask participants to listen without thinking about themselves. Ask them to pay attention, nod, appreciate, confirm, support, and ask questions only to clarify. Take longer for this conversation, about two minutes.

2. Switch roles and repeat the exercise so everyone has the chance to experience listening and being heard.

3. Debrief the exercise. Ask the question "How was that?" Generally, people will like this portion much better and will easily see the difference. Listening leads to a lively and energetic conversation.

Being self-centered is an obstacle to listening. Another major obstacle is indifference. Indifference leads to *pseudolistening.* Do you ever find yourself pretending that you are listening? That is pseudolistening. You look for all intents and purposes like you are listening until that telltale moment when, the speaker asks you a question and you cannot answer because you were not listening to the conversation.

 Facilitator: For humor, you can ask if anyone is pseudolistening right now.

 ## Training Tip: Storytelling

Most adults do not enjoy long lectures. However, they do enjoy a good story, particularly a rousing story that relates powerfully to the topic at hand. For each major point you make, search your life and readings for powerful stories. Practice the skills of storytelling, and become a great teller of tales.[5]

SUMMARY

I hope you have decided to become a more powerful listener. You have heard listening has many benefits. These include insight, professional and personal effectiveness, leadership, understanding and connection with others, and even better health. You have also experienced that people have a deep need for others to listen to them.

The will to listen is like passive volition. It is not something you can force. Rather it is like people who learn to lower their blood pressure using biofeedback. If they try too hard, they get uptight and their blood pressure goes up. When they learn how, they learn to relax, and their blood pressure goes down.

Skills alone do not make you a great listener. We have to draw on a deep desire to understand and connect with other people. Listening takes effort and caring. To listen we must be willing to suspend our point of view for a while, for the sake of understanding someone else. Remarkably, this understanding tends to come back as people understand us, also.

The first step in becoming a great listener is to gain the will to listen. Now we will move to the second element in the powerful listening model, attending.

Element 2. Attending

Time for segment: 40 minutes

Attending is making ourselves available to others by suspending our needs, at least for a while. This process takes an act of will, or volition, as we have described already. But what does it mean to stop and pay attention to another human being?

Attending is mindfulness or awareness. First you need to stop whatever you are doing. Stop word processing. Stop taking calls. Then turn and face the person. Give the person your complete attention.

In attending we do not react; we *act.* We make a decision to pay attention to the other person. In emotional situations, we suspend our defensiveness. We take a break, breathe, and attend completely to the person before us.

Exercise 1.2. Mindfulness

The first exercise with attention is to be mindful. Now, first sit comfortably. Pay attention to your body. How does your body feel? How do you feel emotionally? If you want to, you can stretch. Take a few deep breaths. We are looking for awareness without the mental overload so common in our time. In the literature on organizational learning Senge and others call this state a moment of awareness.[6]

We will do a mindfulness exercise for three minutes. Begin by sitting up comfortably. Put down your pen. Find your center of gravity. Become aware of how you feel and the life around you. During the next three minutes, just breathe. Feel your body and emotions. Be aware of yourself and what is in this room. If your mind drifts off, just bring it gently back.

Ready? I'll let you know when the three minutes are up.

Do the exercise with the participants. When three minutes are up, let them know.

Debrief the exercise. Ask the participants, "What did you experience?" Relate their comments back to the themes of awareness, mindfulness, paying attention. You can mention the Yogi Berra quote "You can see a lot just by looking." In short, to listen well you have to *stop* and give your complete attention to the other person.

There are other features of attending. One is your physical capacity to listen. Many of us have listened to loud music or machines. If you question your hearing, get it checked. Using a hearing aid is better than missing what's going on around you.

Another basic impediment to listening is physical noise. Is the radio playing? Are sirens wailing outside? Turn the radio off. Wait for the ambulances to pass by. Be aware of the physical environment for listening.

Other concerns are more personal. Often our own personal needs monopolize our minds as we ought to be listening. Attending consists of suspending our own personal needs and interests for a while. Our next exercise will address this issue now.

Principles for attending

The next exercise will be a group listening exercise about *attending,* or being mindful of other people as they speak. Psychologist Carl Rogers taught four principles for attending.

 Facilitator: Display and read overhead 1.10.

> *Principles for Attending*
>
> • Empathy
> • Confirmation
> • Nonjudgment
> • Deep listening
>
> 1.10

The first principle is *empathy.* Empathy is often explained with the expression, "Walk a mile in their shoes." In other words, try to feel what it is like to be the other person. I do not know if we can really *feel* what it is like to be another person, but I believe we can *imagine* what it is like to be the other person. Philosopher Martin Buber called this process imagining the real.[7] We can imagine the world of the other and begin to relate to that person. By empathizing, we take the time to imagine and resonate with the world of another person.

The second principle is *confirmation.* In confirmation, we verify the experience of the other person by acknowledging and responding to the other. This response can be nonverbal or verbal. Think about your own need to be heard, which is your own need for confirmation. Feeling heard means that the listener responds. We all want this acknowledgment.

The next principle is being *nonjudgmental,* or what Carl Rogers called unconditional positive regard.[8] Would you feel like sharing your personal world with someone who was judgmental? Of course not! So suspend your evaluation for a while. This stance does not mean that you agree with the person. It does mean that you want simply to understand and support the person's point of view. Later you might want to confront, but for now, you accept the other person's view.

The final principle is *deep listening.* In deep listening we become aware of what is behind a person's words—his or her—emotions, thinking, contradictions, and culture. Often our deeper meanings are not stated literally; we only give hints. We imply rather than explain. Deep listening then involves paying attention to what the other person is experiencing behind the mask of words. Nonverbal communication gives clues—the shaking knees, the expression, the blinks, the nervous smile. Deep listening means observing these cues and attending to the inner life of another— his or her aspirations, hopes, and concerns.

Next, we will practice these principles in a listening exercise.

Exercise 1.3. Talking Stick

This next exercise consists of participants sitting in a circle and taking turns talking. It derives from Native American traditions of dialogue. You can ask the participants if they have seen the movie *Dances with Wolves* with Kevin Costner. A scene in this film portrays Native Americans talking about the coming of the white man and what this means. In the Native American tradition of conversation, they take turns talking and thus give one another their complete attention. The scene from *Dances with Wolves* exemplifies the principles of attention, particularly confirmation and nonjudgment.

Ideally, rearrange the chairs and tables so the participants sit in a circle or square without desks. The exercise does not work if they sit in rows facing in one direction. After everyone is seated, ask them to think for a moment about a question such as, What is important about freedom? Or, What do you value the most? Give them a minute to think and then ask them to stop and focus on listening.

The talking stick is passed from person to person, with each participant getting a chance to hold the stick and speak. Everyone in the group focuses on the speaker.

 Facilitator: You should take a turn, too.

After everyone is done, ask for observations: "What is your evaluation of how we listened? Did listening alter us as a group?" Generally, this exercise will make a group more cohesive. If so, you can relate participants' comments to the idea that *listening improves relationships.* Ask participants to move the chairs back to their original configuration.

 Facilitator: Put up overhead 1.11.

Next we will do an exercise that is more interactive. Active listening involves the principles for attending we have covered already. Active listening also involves four skills, which you can see in over-

Skills for Active Listening

- Stop, look, and listen.
- Use minimal encouragers—"ah, so?"
- Paraphrase—content and feeling.
- Use minimal inquiry.

1.11

head 1.11. The first we have talked about before—mindfulness, or stop, look, and listen. Stop what you are doing. If you have to, ask the person to wait for a moment so you can wind up your current activity and then turn to face him or her. Take a breath and give him or her your full attention.

The second skill is to encourage the other to speak using *minimal encouragers.* These are sounds such as *ah, um, hm,* and brief questions such as "So?" or "And?" Minimal encouragers help people explain their point of view and delve deeper into their concerns.

Encouraging the other to speak takes many forms. One form of minimal encouragement is an express invitation: "What is on your mind?" Another form is nonverbal. For instance, have you ever known a person whose mere presence enables you to express what is in your heart? With others, you would not dream of sharing anything important to you. This feeling is about trust and empathy, or the capacity for caring.

We can also show interest in the other person by feeding back to him what we think was meant. This third skill is *paraphrasing.* You can paraphrase content or feeling. Here is an example of paraphrasing content: "So you believe there are just are not enough resources to make this project a success." Check to see if this paraphrase is accurate. Ask, "Is this what you meant?"

Here is a paraphrase of emotion: "So you feel frustrated and overwhelmed by how this project is being managed?" Again, check for accuracy. Ask, "Is this how you feel?"

The last skill is *minimal inquiry.* Do this step after the person has explained himself or herself and after you have checked your understanding with paraphrases. Rather than respond by sharing your experience, ask the person to explain more and perhaps to consider some solutions. Here are some examples of minimal inquiry:

- So what does it all mean?
- So where does that leave things?
- Have you thought about your options?

Exercise 1.4. Active Listening

Again in this exercise you will work in your pairs. Each partner will have a chance to speak. I would like you to pick some difficulty in your life. This problem can be anything less than perfect in your professional or personal life. It should be something you do not mind sharing. Take a moment to write it down, if it helps.

Give the participants about ten seconds.

Okay. In this exercise the speaker explains his or her difficulty while the other partner practices the skills we just covered. I will leave the overhead up as a reminder. You can take a break during the exercise and refer to the skills. Make sure you use them all—stop, look, and listen; minimal encouragers; paraphrasing content and emotion; and minimal inquiry. The first conversation will last three minutes. Then we will debrief and switch roles. Any questions? Okay, decide who will go first. Each speaker has three minutes.

After three minutes, ask those who spoke to give feedback to the listeners. Prod them, asking, "Did the listener follow the active listening principles and skills? What advice does the speaker have for the listener?" Then repeat the exercise with the roles reversed. Have the partners debrief again.

Finally, debrief the entire exercise. Ask, "What was your experience with active listening?" Summarize the exercise with the following themes:

- Active listening generates powerful conversations.
- Active listening generates connectivity between people.

Summary

So far in this session, we covered two elements in the powerful listening cycle—volition and attention. We discussed the benefits of listening in our lives and how to become more aware of others in our conversations. The next element in the powerful listening model is understanding.

Element 3. Understanding

Time for segment: 35 minutes

 Facilitator: Begin the instruction by showing overheads 1.12 and 13. Read the quotes.

Listening *is* perception—a natural process that often leads to misunderstanding. If we want to understand other people, we have to overcome natural problems such as projection, defensiveness, emotional reaction, giving advice, and supportiveness. We will explore these problems with the process of perception.

Perception Quotes

"Listen to me for a day . . . an hour! . . . a moment! Lest I expire in my lonely silence? O God, is there no one to listen?"

—Seneca

1.12

Perception Quotes (Cont.)

"You and I do not see things as they are. We see things as we are."

—Herb Cohen

1.13

Facilitator: Show overhead 1.14.

Perception

1.14

Overhead 1.14 shows a graphic that can be seen two different ways. Ask participants what they see. Some will see one thing; some, something else; and yet others will go back and forth between the two views. Ask people to look at the picture until they can easily move between the two perceptions of the same graphic.

The overhead demonstrates how the mind organizes information during perception. *Perception* is a process through which our minds color our world. Perception is not a passive process whereby we accurately make sense of what is outside us. Perception is a creative process whereby we select, organize, and interpret information.

In listening, perception begins when we select what we hear. Have you ever felt sensitive about something personal? Then when you are out in a crowd, do you think you hear someone talking about this very thing or you pick out your name from the background noise? These are examples of selective perception, or *selective listening.* We project a great deal when we listen. We project on other people our preconceptions, our needs, and our biases. Perception, then, is often *inferential.* We select and fit what we perceive into what we already know—categories, stereotypes, mental models, and opinions.

Powerful listening requires taking a break from our mental models and preconceptions. One of the hardest times to overcome our mental models is during conflict, particularly when we have a difficult emotional history with someone.

In our next activity, we will explore the most difficult listening situation—an emotionally charged incident. We will do this exercise because we learn from difficult situations. First, I would like you to remember a conversation that was emotionally difficult for you. Most of us can remember at least one. Turn to activity 1.1 in your workbook, and complete steps 1 and 2. Leave step 3 for later. This exercise is private. You don't have to share this story with anyone else. Don't take long. You have four minutes.

 Facilitator: Review workbook activity 1.1.

OVERCOMING OBSTACLES TO UNDERSTANDING

Identify a conversation in which you felt defensive. This could be in your personal or professional life. Often, such a reaction occurs when you have a negative emotional history with someone. Somehow this person knew how to aggravate you or "push your buttons."

Step 1. The Critical Incident

In the space below write a brief description of the last time you felt defensive in a conversation. *Defensiveness* is an emotional reaction where one feels attacked and vulnerable. This conversation could have occurred at work or in your social or personal life.

A critical incident where you felt attacked or vulnerable:

Step 2. Your Experience

Analyze this experience. In the space below describe your experience.

Your experience of the conversation—your emotional reaction:

Step 3. A More Effective Response

Next, consider how you could have behaved differently. In the space below, describe a more effective response.

How you could have handled this situation differently:

Wait four minutes, and then direct the group.

Please take a few moments to finish your writing. Now I am going to ask you to share some of your feelings about this conversation. You do not have to share the actual details.

Go through the questions on the handout. Relate responses to the themes of disconnection, strong emotion, poor listening, and misunderstanding.

We often react emotionally when we interact with others in a difficult situation. This response is natural but usually not productive. A gut-level reaction does not lead to understanding. This instantaneous gut reaction is what our ancestors felt when confronted with a threat—sweating hands, racing heart, and adrenaline pumping. It works well for a fight-or-flight response, but it does not serve us well in conversation.

In *The Lost Art of Listening* psychologist Michael Nichols says, "Most failures of understanding are not due to self-absorption or bad faith, but to defensive reactions that crowd out understanding and concern. . . . To become better listeners . . . we must identify and harness the emotional triggers that generate anxiety and cause misunderstanding."[9] This ability to gain control of and suspend our reaction is a great art. Again, we must make the distinction between reaction and action. To suspend our defensiveness and needs for a while is a creative act on behalf of the relationship.

 Facilitator: Show overheads 1.15 and 1.16.

Explain the items on overheads 1.15 and 1.16. Emphasize that although these reactions are evident in conflicts, they also play a part in less dramatic relationships.

Dramatic episodes are instructive of how we can become better listeners. Problems of perception occur in four areas.

The first problem is emotional reaction and defensiveness. As Michael Nichols said, "Reacting emotionally to what another person says is the number-one reason conversations turn into arguments."[10] *Defensiveness* is the perception of hostility from another party. Of course, some-

---

Problems of Perception

- Reacting emotionally and defensively.
  - Reactionary tactics:
    - Attacking
    - Ambushing
    - Monopolizing
    - Avoiding

1.15

Problems of Perception (Cont.)

- Self-interested listening:
  - Selective listening
  - Literal listening
  - Filling in the gaps
  - Assimilating into prior understanding
- Giving advice.
- Offering support instead of listening.

1.16

times people *are* hostile, and recognizing that distinction is important. However, many times we perceive people as more hostile than they really are, and our reaction makes things worse. Our reaction contributes to the misunderstanding whereas a master listener would add clarity to the situation.

Based on our emotional reaction we often respond with one of the following knee-jerk tactics.

- *Attacking.* In attacking we find the speakers' weakest points in order to defeat them.
- *Ambushing.* Ambushing is listening to the content of what people say and then using their own words or arguments against them. Then we can defeat them logically.
- *Monopolizing.* By interrupting or continuously talking, we simply do not let others speak.
- *Avoiding.* By avoiding, we fail to learn, to inquire, or to respond to our conversational partner.

Another problem area in perception is self-interested listening, which takes several forms.

- *Selective listening.* This form is when we actually do not hear what others say. We simply miss it altogether. Also, selective listening can take the form of not remembering what others say.
- *Literal listening.* Here we listen for the literal content of what the other person says, but we miss the underlying emotion, purpose, or meaning of the statement. People are not always articulate, clear, or straightforward.
- *Filling in the gaps.* This problem occurs when we supply our own additional information to what someone says. Unfortunately, the information we supply is often wrong.
- *Assimilating to prior understanding.* Here we project our own experiences and inferences into the communication of others. In our minds, our mental models become the substance of what someone else is trying to say.

Overhead 1.15 lists two more problems that interfere with understanding—advice giving and supportiveness. Both of these well-intentioned behaviors often are not effective. For example, we want to give advice to help other people resolve their difficulties; however, our advice giving preempts their self-expression and often our understanding of their point of view. The same is true of supportiveness. Saying, "Cheer up, everything is going to be okay" can be a source of disconnection. Such a comment invalidates how the other person feels. Even though it might seem counterintuitive, to reassure someone means you are not listening to him or her. The times for advice and reassurance come after listening, when the other person is ready for assurance.

Many internal barriers to understanding have to do with perception and defensiveness and with our misguided need to give advice and to reassure. Happily, overcoming these barriers is simple. First, suspend your reaction. As Michael Nichols explains, "The act of listening requires a submersion of the self and immersion in the other."[11] Second, ask what the other person thinks. To be successful use empathy.

 Facilitator: Return to workbook activity 1.1.

Ask the participants to return to the workbook activity and to complete step 3. Give them two minutes. Circulate and help people who seem stuck. When they are done, continue.

What ideas did you come up with to deal with this situation differently in the future? Learning to deal well with difficult situations is a distinguishing feature of a powerful listener.

If some participants mention asking questions as a more effective response, relate their ideas to the next topic of asking questions.

The art of asking questions

The art of asking questions builds on the skills we learned in exercise 1-4 on active listening. This simple method of asking questions, however, is difficult to remember in emotional conversations. Here it is: When you encounter a difficult emotional situation, first take a deep breath, and then ask a question with as much empathy as you can. Formulate your question with your best guess about the other person's point of view. Start from where the other person is. Your question ought to help him take one step in explaining his experience.

Although it might sound easy, asking the right question at the right time for the right person is a great art that few have mastered. So let us study this art.

Socrates is acknowledged as the father of the rhetorical question. About 2,400 years ago, Socrates and the leaders of Athens argued about whether a slave could learn philosophy or mathematics. Socrates decided to demonstrate his argument on the spot. He called forth a slave and decided to teach him the Pythagorean theorem. The remarkable thing is that Socrates taught this theorem successfully to the slave using only questions.

Socrates' questions, however, later got him into trouble with Athens' leaders. This distinction is the first we will make in the art of asking questions: Some questions cause trouble. As we just discussed in the problem of reactionary tactics, we can use questions to ambush people. A question asked in a mocking tone—"Do you really believe that your project can make any money?"—can undermine a conversation.

Good questions, on the other hand, increase understanding. They do not provoke hostility. The criterion for a good question is simple: It should help the other person explain his point of view in his own terms.

 Facilitator: Show and read overhead 1.17.[12]

Asking Questions

- Purposes:
  - Reducing uncertainty
  - Connecting and finding mutuality
  - Checking perceptions
  - Overcoming the problems of perception and misunderstanding

1.17

Questions reduce uncertainty by opening up communication where it was closed. Questions connect us with others and uncover our mutuality. They help us check our perceptions. In short, questions overcome the problems of perception and misunderstanding.

 Facilitator: Display overheads 1.18 and 1.19, and review the nature of questions.

Features of Questions

- Two types are open- and closed-ended.
- Open-ended questions help the other to learn, express, and evaluate.
- Empathic questions show concern.
- Questions check inferences.

1.18

- Use *open- and closed-ended questions.* "What were revenues last year?" is a closed-ended question, because it prompts a very short, predictable answer. An open-ended question—for example, "What is your evaluation of last year's revenues?"—invites a person to explain his or her point of view.

- *Show concern with empathic questions.* Empathy is a requirement for effective listening. Care about and inquire into how the other person thinks and feels.

- *Check inferences.* As you come to what you believe is an understanding of the other person's

Features of Questions (Cont.)

- Probes help the other express his deeper concerns, solve problems, gain perspective.
- Patiently wait for answers.
- Avoid using argumentative questions.
- Avoid putting down the other's answers.
- Appreciation of answers is crucial.

1.19

views, realize that your understanding is still only a guess, or an inference. Confirm your understanding by asking questions.

- *Probe.* Try to get a deeper understanding. Ask how the other party feels about the situation. Ask for an example or a story for clarification. Ask about the implications of what he or she is describing ("What other effects might this have?") and about what actions he or she might have considered.

• *Show appreciation and patience.* Wait for the person to respond. Give him or her time to think as well as your appreciation. You can confront the person with differences later. Now it is time to understand his or her point of view.

Asking good questions enables us to understand people on their own terms. This effort is one of the greatest gifts we can give to another person.

Exercise 1.5. The Questions Game

Now it is time for another exercise. Again we will work in pairs, and we will take turns as speakers and as listeners. This exercise has a clear objective—to keep the other person talking as long as possible by asking great questions. How long can you keep the other person talking? Perhaps you have seen the bumper sticker, "He who dies with the most toys wins." Actually, in human relationships and in this exercise, those who ask the most good questions win.

In your pairs, decide who is going to speak first and who will ask questions and listen. I will stop you after four minutes. Then you will reverse roles. Any questions?

Have the speakers switch roles after four minutes. Observe the participants. Intervene if someone stops asking questions and the exchange becomes more like a simple conversation.

Debrief the exercise. Ask the participants what it was like to do the question game. Who won? Who asked great questions? Relate their responses back to the theme of understanding others on their own terms.

Summary

Understanding is rare among people. We tend to believe understanding happens more than it really does. As Michael Nichols says, "Listening is so basic that we take it for granted. Unfortunately, most of us think of ourselves as better listeners than we really are."[13] So far in the workshop, we have covered the first three elements of the powerful listening model—volition, attending, and understanding.

Midpoint Break

Time for break: 15 minutes

Clearly state your expectations about starting on time after the break. Tell the participants that after the break you will cover the last three features of the model—memory, responding, and development.

Element 4. Memory

Time for segment: 25 minutes

A good memory is a sign of healthy listening. Of course, remembering what people say can be difficult. Research shows that we tend to forget more than half of what people tell us as soon as we hear it. We remember only about one-third of a message after eight hours, and only 25 percent after two months.[14] Establishing a powerful memory takes effort and practice, and it can be developed.

Tell a story from your own experience to reinforce the point. Here's an example:

> Recently, I met with a neighbor of mine who is a manager in a major corporation. I could tell that he needed to improve his listening and his memory.
>
> We talked about the food we were supposed to bring to a social gathering. At the end of our conversation, he repeated what we each were slotted to bring. I have high standards for listening, and for me the reiteration seemed to have a downside. Repeating the commitments is not necessarily poor communication; however, if we listen and remember well, then repetition is unnecessary. In fact, repetition can reinforce poor listening. We say to ourselves, "Why should I listen when this will be repeated?" I noticed later at the social gathering that my neighbor had indeed forgotten what we each had agreed to bring.
>
> Memory is an important area of development. In his *Page-a-Minute Memory Book,* H. Lorayne declares, "There is no such thing as a poor memory! There are only trained and untrained memories."[15]
>
> There are two problems to overcome in training our memories. The first is simply forgetting important things. Overcoming that obstacle is relatively easy—we train ourselves. The other problem is that over time our memories tend to distort things. That obstacle is harder to overcome.

Have you ever noticed how convenient memory can be? We remember some things and not others, often in response to our own self-interest. The challenge is to retain information accurately.

Facilitator: Show overhead 1.20.

Ways to Improve Memory

- Use association.
- Identify and isolate messages.
- Generate priorities.
- Create a structure.
- Use repetition and rehearsal.

1.20

Here are some guidelines for memory.

Use association. If you are trying to remember someone's name, stop for a while and make an association with something you already know. You might know someone else who has the same name, for example. Association involves ingenuity. You have to create your own associations. With association, a mental picture is often easier to remember than words. For example, if you want to remember a specific task you want to do in the future, see yourself doing that task.

Identify and select out important messages from the mass of information that forms the background. Information overload is now a problem in all of our lives. We all need to spend some time consciously picking out and memorizing important information.

Extract ideas and structure rather than trying to memorize everything. This skill is similar to taking notes. Identify the important points and memorize them.

Use repetition and rehearsal to improve your memory. Repeat important information to yourself immediately after you hear it. This repetition helps move messages from short- to long-term memory.

Use mnemonics or other structures to organize ideas into memory. You could use a series of percentages or a series of letters. For example, we can use the acronym VAUMRD to represent the elements in the powerful listening model.

Exercise 1.6. The Memory Game

In this game, participants recall what others have said so far in the session. Adapt your questions to the group. Some groups are much more familiar with one another. Consequently, asking them to remember one another's names is not difficult enough. In that event, make the game more challenging.

Here are the directions for the basic game. First, have people go around the room with their name tents, attempting to memorize the names of other people. Encourage them to invent an association for each person they do not know. Then, ask people to hide their name tents. Go around the room with each person saying the name of every other person in the circle. Continue until everyone knows all of the names.

In a modification of this game ask all the participants to recall whatever personal information each person has shared so far—hobbies, interests, stories. Yet another modification is to ask each person to identify the name and something personal about the person to their right. Then others in the group can add details that the speaker might have forgotten. Usually, this game is fun, and it demonstrates how well people have listened thus far.

Summary

The good news about memory is that we do tend to remember our impressions of other people, particularly those we care about. Remembering what other people tell us is a message to them that we care. I know some successful politicians—a U.S. senator, for example—who have phenomenal memories for people's names, even remembering someone's name they met once years earlier. No wonder they are successful politicians. The elements in the powerful listening model are not mutually exclusive—each contains all the others. Memory involves all phases of the listening cycle—it takes volition, it occurs while attending and understanding, and by showing someone that you remember important information, it is a form of response to another person.

Element 5. Responding

Time for segment: 40 minutes

 Facilitator: Prepare a flip chart. Write "Types of responses" at the top.

A good way to introduce this segment is by telling a story. However, before you tell the story, inform the participants that they will be asked to explain how they would respond in the situation described.

Here is an example story.

> Recently, I was working at my computer, and I had a call from a friend, Susan. She asked me if I had a few moments to hear about her predicament. I stopped what I was doing and said sure. Susan told me that one of her associates, Bob, had just hung up on her. Susan said she had accidentally scheduled two meetings at the same time and had left a voice mail message with Bob canceling her meeting with him. Bob missed the message and showed up at Susan's office. When Bob didn't find Susan, he made a scene and left. Later, on the phone, Bob had hung up on her.
>
> Susan was clearly upset. She said that Bob was an influential person in the organization. Susan was asking me for help. I needed to respond, but how?

Ask the participants how they would respond to Susan. Write their responses on the flip chart. Write down a one-word description of the type of response each person suggests. Many of these suggestions can fit into the types of responses covered in this section:

- Passivity
- Questions
- Paraphrases
- Empathy
- Advice
- Feedback
- Assessment
- Confrontation

Acknowledge and summarize the participants' responses. Then introduce the next topic—selecting the appropriate response.

> In deciding how to respond the important first step is listening to yourself. While you are listening to another, ask yourself, "How do I feel right at this moment?" If you don't ask yourself this question, then you risk reaction. When I was listening to Susan, for instance, I felt a sponta-

neous gut reaction—it was almost as if I took Bob's attack on her personally, and I wanted to comfort and support her. The first rule in responding, however, is *not to react.* Instead, think and then act. Usually the best response is not to offer reactive advice, assessment, or support.

The most appropriate response is usually to ask a question, get more information, and then paraphrase. I took these steps with Susan's problem. Then Susan asked me for an assessment and advice, both of which I offered, I tried to help her gain a larger perspective on her problem. I reminded Susan that mistakes are inevitable and a source of learning. I suggested she contact Bob again later to apologize and shore up the relationship. Then I focused on empathy and support. By the way, this story had a happy ending. Bob called Susan back and admitted he was just having a bad day, and they rescheduled the meeting.

 Facilitator: Show overhead 1.21.

The first four ways of responding have been covered already in the workshop—passivity, paraphrasing, questions, and empathy and support. Using examples, explain the upside and downside of each way of responding.

Eight Ways of Responding
1. Passivity
2. Paraphrasing
3. Questions
4. Support
5. Advice
6. Feedback
7. Assessment
8. Confrontation
1.21

Response	Upside	Downside
Passivity	Hearing	Alone does not ensure understanding
Paraphrases	Understanding	Presumptuous
Questions	Understanding	Tone can provoke hostility
Support	Connection	Support can bypass another's concerns
Advice	Path forward	Disconnection if person is not ready
Feedback	Insight	Disconnection if given poorly
Assessment	Perspective	Alienation
Confrontation	Learning	Alienation

We must carefully weigh our options. In *passivity,* we simply listen and do not probe for understanding. In questioning and paraphrasing, we gain understanding, but as we have discussed, the other party can regard our questions as hostile and our paraphrasing as presumptuous, especially if we do not try to empathize. Supportiveness builds connection, but it can bypass the speaker's concerns and need to be heard.

By giving advice, we help a person find a direction and a path forward. By giving feedback, we provide people with a simple picture of what they are doing. However, both advice and feedback can alienate the speaker if they are given poorly or if the speaker is not ready to hear them. Sometimes the speaker does not want or benefit from someone else's *assessment,* or the objective evaluation of the person and his or her situation. In confrontation, our experiences and interests clash with those of our partner. From this process, we can learn from each other, but our differences can also lead to alienation.

Now, we are going to explore these eight responses in an exercise. Do you have any questions about the eight types of responses? Can you identify them in a conversation?

Exercise 1.7. Eight Ways of Responding

In this exercise, the participants take turns speaking, responding, and observing the eight different responses in conversations. The participants record their observation using workbook activity 1.2.

 Facilitator: Review workbook activity 1.2.

1. Form participants into teams of four people each.

2. Assign the roles of speaker, listener-responder, and two observers per team. The *speaker* will select a real-life problem he or she is willing to discuss. The *listener-responder* will respond to the problem. The two *observers* will use the observation sheet in workbook activity 1.2.

3. The speaker and listener-responder converse for three minutes.

4. The two observers mark the types of responses given in their workbooks.

5. The observers and speakers give feedback to the listener-responder. What types of responses did the listener-responder use? How effective were they?

6. Repeat with the two observers switching roles with the speaker and the listener-responder. The exercise will be repeated only once.

7. Debrief the exercise as a whole. Which responses did people tend to use? How effective were they?

The participants might identify questions, paraphrasing, and support as most effective. If people had difficulty with advice, feedback, assessment, and confrontation, then that observation is a good transition to the next sections on advice and feedback. Confrontation will be covered in greater detail in module 2 on assertiveness and module 3 on conflict management.

 TRAINING TIP: MANAGING TIME

At this point plan out the time remaining for the session. Check the time. You need about twenty-five minutes for the final section on development. If you

EIGHT WAYS OF RESPONDING

Complete the sheet below for the conversation that you observe. Put a check in the appropriate box each time the listener-responder uses one of the ways of responding.

Listening Observation 1									
Passivity									
Paraphrasing									
Questions									
Support									
Advice									
Feedback									
Assessment									
Confrontation									

Listening Observation 2									
Passivity									
Paraphrasing									
Questions									
Support									
Advice									
Feedback									
Assessment									
Confrontation									

are short on time, read the three overheads for advice and feedback quickly. However, if you have extra time, then you can go more slowly.

Giving Advice

Giving someone a direction or advice can be a dangerous tactic. Research has shown that directive responses are often unproductive, particularly in cases of bereavement, or when someone is suffering a personal loss.

 Facilitator: Display and explain overheads 1.22 and 1.23.

> *Giving Advice*
>
> • Upside:
>   • Giving advice can provide people with a path forward.
>   • Giving advice that people want and can use benefits them.
> • Downside:
>   • Giving advice prematurely might alienate the recipients.
>   • Giving unsolicited advice wastes everyone's time.
>
> 1.22

> *Giving Advice (Cont.)*
>
> • Guidelines:
>   • Make sure you are giving advice in order to benefit others, not yourself.
>   • Wait until you understand those involved and the situation.
>   • Wait for a teachable moment.
>   • Wait until they ask for it.
>   • Use their aspirations and help them accomplish their goals.
>   • Give advice about one step they can take.
>
> 1.23

Giving advice can be problematic. An obvious problem is someone might fail as a result of your advice. You have to learn to give advice wisely. Advice is premature when: (1) the others do not trust you; (2) they do not feel understood, or your advice-giving keeps them from explaining themselves; and (3) they do not want advice.

Some people want advice. The first step in advice-giving is to listen and understand the problem. Sense if others really want advice. If you sense they do, then you can ask them if they want your guidance. Only then should you offer your advice. Keep it short, and as far as possible, let them make their own decisions. Pay attention to their views on their terms, and check back later to see whether your advice was helpful.

Explain the guidelines for advice on the overhead. Provide stories where appropriate. Then outline the benefits of giving advice. Sometimes we can give advice to someone and it really helps. Encourage the participants to watch their advice-giving in real-life conversations. Using the guidelines, they should notice when they are successful and when they are resisted.

Move on to the next topic, which is feedback.

Feedback

Feedback is similar to advice—it is easy for people to resist. Often, however, powerful listening requires a powerful response. Feedback is a powerful response that can complete the process of listening. In giving feedback, we play back conversations so others can hear their own communication. The word *feedback,* incidentally, comes from information theory in electronics. Technically, feedback is a return of some of the output signal as input.

Of course, feedback has its problems. If the speaker anticipates negative feedback or, worse yet, that he might be punished in some fashion for his views, then he might withhold information.

 Facilitator: Prepare two flip-chart pages. On the first one, write "Worst feedback," and on the other, write "Best feedback."

Ask the participants for the best and worst feedback they remember receiving. Begin with the worst. Probe for stories and put their responses on the flip chart.

Next, ask the participants for the characteristics of the best feedback they have received.

When giving feedback, be direct and not judgmental. Give an accurate response without encouraging defensiveness. For feedback to be heard, we need to establish a nondefensive climate.

Defensiveness is a shroudlike cover over the conversation. The understanding and mutuality you work all along to establish through empathic listening can be destroyed.

 Facilitator: Show and explain overheads 1.24 and 1.25. Use the participants' stories to explain that effective feedback does not arouse defensiveness.

Defensive Behaviors

- Evaluation of others or their ideas
- Attempt to control the conversation or situation
- Use of strategy or concealed motivations
- Neutrality and noninvolvement
- Certainty or dogmatism

1.24

 Facilitator: Next, display and read overheads 1.26 and 1.27.

Supportive Behaviors

- Nonjudgmental description
- A problem orientation that is not imposing
- Spontaneity or noncalculating behavior
- Empathy with the speaker
- Equality based on mutual trust and respect

1.25

Alternate option. If time warrants, you can conduct an exercise in which the participants take turns giving one another feedback. The objective is to follow the guidelines on overheads 1.24 through 1.27.

Ask the participants to form into pairs. The people in the feedback-giver roles design a role-play based on a real-life situation in which they would like to give someone feedback. The feedback-givers inform their partners of the situation. The listeners' role is mostly passive, with the listener being attentive and saying little. Allow two minutes for the exercise, and then debrief. Repeat the exercise, with the roles reversed, so everyone gets a chance to give feedback and to listen. Ask the participants about how well they were able to follow the guidelines and about how well the feedback worked.

Another version of this exercise involves asking the participants to write the feedback first and then role-play some examples in front of the class. Having an alternative version allows you to adjust for time constraints and to adapt to the participants' needs.

Summary

Listening is an interactive, not passive, process. Any listening that leads to true dialogue is a response to the whole situation.

Every relationship or conversation has three features—yourself, another person, and the situation, or the context, in which the interaction takes place. Powerful listening means listening to all three—to yourself, to others, and to life. By listening to all three, you can discover an appropriate response. The major influences when responding to another person are your common interests along with the interests of the larger whole—your business, for example. Listening for mutuality and for a fit with others in a particular context makes for a powerful conversation.

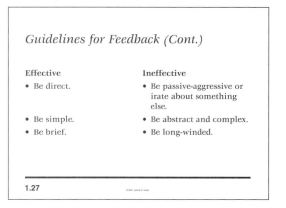

Element 6. Development

Time for segment: 25 minutes

Quickly review the powerful listening model. Next, help the participants transfer what they have learned to their ongoing development in listening.

 Facilitator: Show overhead 1.28.

Listening—the communication activity we engage in most—is the activity we spend the least time studying. Listening is the source of connectivity and power in organizations, yet we

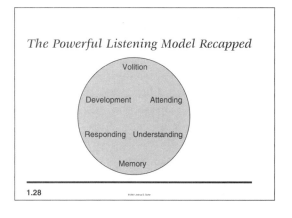

sometimes forget and ignore people. The good news is that the knowledge, skills, and motivation required for powerful listening are learnable and teachable.

 Facilitator: Show overhead 1.29.

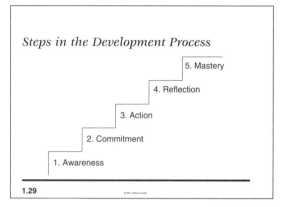

Explain the steps or levels of development in overhead 1.29. These steps pertain to any communication skill.

The first or bottom level, *awareness,* is when we discover our need to develop our listening skills. We realize that by becoming better listeners we can improve our work relationships and performance. This level leads to the next, where we make a *commitment* to development. We study the topic, read books, and attend workshops. More important, we pay attention to listening in our everyday conversations.

The third level involves *action.* We practice the skills and insights of attending, understanding, remembering, and responding in our actual conversations. In the next level, *reflection,* we monitor the results of our work, and we think on these conversations and relationships. We take the time to determine what does and does not work for us. Then we translate what we learn from reflection into improving our practice, our listening, our conversations, and our relationships.

We become reliable listeners through our practice and work. One great thing about development is that it works. Listening is definitely learnable.

 Facilitator: Tell a story about someone you know who learned how to listen and how gaining this skill served as a breakthrough for that person.

In many instances people have undertaken development in communication and have made major breakthroughs. The top level in the development process is *mastery,* which means you have a teachable point of view about listening. In other words, around you, other people learn how to listen, also. They notice your listening skills and ask you to coach them. You become a powerful force for generating listening in your organization.

Ask participants to complete workbook activity 1.3 in their workbooks. This task establishes their personal plan for ongoing development in listening. Explain the process for filling out the workbook activity. The workbook provides space to write two goals. Encourage the participants to complete at least one. Give them six minutes to work.

DEVELOPMENT PLAN FOR LISTENING

Reflect on the skills and attitudes you have studied in this workshop. Answer the question, What development area in listening would be a breakthrough for me? Work with the first step in the development process—awareness. Brainstorm answers in the space below. All possibilities are good possibilities.

Possible development areas:

_____

_____

_____

_____

_____

_____

_____

_____

_____

_____

_____

Next select an area for development. Consider the following criteria.

- The development goal would be a *breakthrough* for you in your relationships with others.
- The goal is *concrete*—you and others could observe whether you perform the behavior.
- The *results* of the goal are observable, too. If you integrate the behavior in your life, you can observe the positive effects on others and in your relationships.
- You select the goal freely and feel an *internal commitment* toward this goal.

Write your goal on the following form. Use more paper if needed.

Development Area 1

Your goal for development in listening:

_____

_____

_____

Why you have selected this goal:

_____

_____

_____

How you will accomplish this goal (include research, plans, behaviors):

_____

_____

_____

Others who can help you accomplish this goal:

_____

_____

_____

How you will follow up and know if you are successful:

_____

_____

_____

_____

_____

_____

Development Area 2

Your goal for development in listening:

_____

_____

_____

Why you have selected this goal:

_____

_____

_____

How you will accomplish this goal (include research, plans, behaviors):

_____

_____

_____

Others who can help you accomplish this goal:

_____

_____

_____

How you will follow up and know if you are successful:

_____

_____

_____

_____

_____

_____

_____

Facilitator: Review workbook activity 1.3.

Exercise 1.8. Working with a Partner

Invite participants to share the details of their development plan with a partner. Tell them they have four minutes for this activity and that you will let them know at halftime so both partners have a chance to share.

Alternate Option. As a stand-alone session, ask the participants to set up future meetings with their partners for follow-up sessions. As development partners, they will meet again, at least on the phone, between one and two weeks after the workshop and debrief regarding progress toward their goals. Instruct them to write their partner's name and phone number and the date(s) on which they will reconnect on their development plans.

Summary

Time for segment: 5 minutes

You are ready to end the session. Ask the participants, "What did we cover in this session that you will find useful in your work?" Go around the room and ask each person what he or she learned in the session. Allow time for discussion.

Listening is the foundation of interpersonal communication. We could say that listening is the source of any kind of effective communication. As the ancient writer, Zeno of Cintium, once observed, "We have been given two ears and but a single mouth, in order that we might hear more and talk less."

End the session with relevant logistical details. For example, if the participants are breaking for lunch, encourage them to practice their listening skills during their lunchtime conversations.

NOTES

1. D. Borisoff and M. Purdy, *Listening in Everyday Life: A Personal and Professional Approach,* 2d ed. (New York: University Press in America, 1996), 4.
2. L. Barker, C. Edwards, K. G. Gaines, and F. Holley, "An Investigation of Proportional Time Spent in Various Communication Activities by College Students," *Journal of Applied Communication Research* 8 (1981): 101–9.
3. T. J. Peters, *In Search of Excellence: Lessons from America's Best-Run Companies* (New York: Warner Books, 1988), 196.
4. Borisoff and Purdy, *Listening in Everyday Life,* and J. T. Wood, *Interpersonal Communication: Everyday Encounters,* 2d ed. (Belmont, CA: Wadsworth, 1999), chapter 6.
5. See, for example, R. Collins and P. J. Cooper, *The Power of Story: Teaching through Storytelling,* 2d ed. (New York: Prentice Hall, 1996), and J. Slan, *Using Stories and Humor: Grab Your Audience* (Needham Heights, MA: Allyn & Bacon, 1998).

6. P. Senge, C. Roberts, R. B. Ross, B. J. Smith, and A. Kleiner, *The Fifth Discipline Fieldbook* (New York: Currency Doubleday, 1994), 216.

7. M. Buber, *The Knowledge of Man,* ed. M. Freedman, trans. R. G. Smith (New York: Harper & Row, 1965).

8. Carl R. Rogers, *A Way of Being* (Boston, MA: Houghton Mifflin Company, 1980).

9. M. Nichols, *The Lost Art of Listening,* The Guilford Family Therapy Series (New York: Guilford Press, 1995), 3.

10. Nichols, *The Lost Art of Listening,* 93.

11. Nichols, *The Lost Art of Listening,* 62.

12. See R. B. Adler, L. B. Rosenfeld, and N. Towne, *Interplay: The Process of Interpersonal Communication,* 7th ed. (New York: Harcourt Brace, 1998), for more information on questions.

13. Nichols, *The Lost Art of Listening,* 11.

14. Julia T. Wood, *Interpersonal Communication Everyday Encounters,* 2d ed. (Belmont, CA: Wadsworth Publishing Company, 1999).

15. H. Lorayne, *Page-a-Minute Memory Book* (New York: Ballantine, 1996), 56.

ASSERTIVENESS

INTRODUCTION

This module builds on the foundation established in module 1, "Powerful Listening." Module 2 provides participants with skills, knowledge, and motivation for interpersonal assertiveness, influence, and advocacy. The participants practice skills for the powerful expression that leads to collaboration and effective interaction with others.

INSTRUCTOR PREPARATION

The prerequisite for teaching this session reflects its major theme, *assertiveness,* or the ability to stand up for your rights and interests. Another theme is *appreciation,* which helps people to listen to you because they feel you acknowledge and understand them. It leads to the module's third theme of *influence* or persuasion. Review your own development in these competencies before teaching this session. See chapter 6 for research and further information regarding personal development in assertiveness.

As the instructor you are a model for the workshop participants. Your own voice, assertiveness, and ability to persuade teach volumes. Take a thorough inventory of your own background and competence, and prepare yourself accordingly.

 **Materials**

Assemble the following materials before the session.

❑ Overhead transparencies or slide show for module 2 and appropriate equipment

❑ Two flip-chart pads on easels with markers

❑ Flip-chart pages prepared with content and titles

❑ Three-by-five-inch index cards prepared for the Picture Game (see exercise 2.1); because you give each team different cards, you only have one set for the whole class

❑ Participant workbooks

❑ Trainer's workshop guide

❑ Spoons, hard boiled eggs, oil, and paper towels for the slippery egg relay exercise (see exercise 2.2)

❑ Participant awards for winning games in exercises 2.1 and 2.2

Facilitator: Show overhead 2.1 as participants arrive. Full-size overheads are found in appendix A.

Checklist

Check the facility carefully before the participants arrive.

❑ Does the equipment work?

❑ Are tables and chairs arranged appropriately?

❑ Are windows, doors, and lighting comfortable?

❑ If the break includes refreshments, are they set up?

❑ Do you know the location of rest rooms and telephones?

❑ Do you know the numbers and contacts for emergency assistance?

❑ Are the flip charts set up with markers?

❑ Are name tents available with markers?

Assertiveness

Powerful skills for assertiveness, authenticity, and advocacy

2.1

Scope and Sequence

This session begins with an interactive exercise called the picture game, which demonstrates expressiveness in communication. Next, you will lead the participants in an exercise to appreciate and to encourage others. Along with listening, these skills form guidelines for dialogue and for building relationships.

Skills for assertiveness—for example, asking for what you want and self-confidence—are reinforced with additional exercises. The next section on advocacy shows how to build support for one's ideas in an organization. The session ends with the participants writing personal plans for developing their competence in assertiveness and advocacy.

LECTURE NOTES: ASSERTIVENESS

Total time: **4 hours**
Midpoint break: **15 minutes**

Introduction

Time for segment: 25 minutes

 Facilitator: Show and read overheads 2.2 and 2.3: Module Agenda.

You need a powerful introduction to the work in module 2. Emphasize the following points:

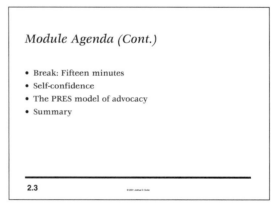

- Interpersonal communication consists of two major elements—listening and speaking.

- Being a good speaker has always been honored, with supporting evidence dating to the ancient Greeks, for example, who valued the intelligent person speaking well.

- Numerous research studies show interpersonal influence is a top requirement for effective leadership.[1]

- Studies also report that being a competent speaker is a prerequisite for success in all spheres—from having the basic communication skills for landing a job to being persuasive enough to become the chief executive officer (CEO).[2]

Also, consider telling an illustrative story at the beginning of the module to hook your listeners. This story could be personal—describe when you first asserted yourself successfully—or about someone who initiated a project and accomplished great things.

Facilitator: Show and read overhead 2.4: Module Objectives.

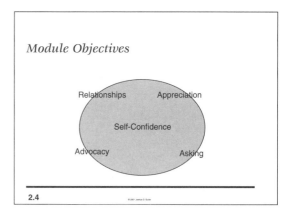

The five features of assertiveness are relationship, appreciation, self-confidence, asking, and advocacy. The module's objective is to develop the participants' understanding of and competence with each of these features.

Next, the module involves the participants in an experiential exercise by playing the picture game.

Exercise 2.1. The Picture Game

We are going to play a game. You have probably played similar games in the past, but you probably did not notice the role that communication plays in these games. I will ask you to observe the different types of communication modeled here and the role that verbal and nonverbal expressiveness plays in winning the game.

 Facilitator: Display overhead 2.5, which details the rules for the game. Read the rules to the participants. Leave the overhead up for the participants' reference.

> *Picture Game Rules*
>
> - Form into groups.
> - Select team names.
> - Decide who draws first.
> - Win points by guessing the drawing.
> - The team with the most points wins a prize.
>
> 2.5

Form the participants into teams. Teams of four or five work best. Have the participants meet in a place designated for each team. Instruct them to pick names for their groups.

 Facilitator: Meanwhile, prepare both flip charts. On the first, you will record the scores, and the teams will draw on the other.

After two minutes, ask each group for its name. Record these on a flip-chart page. Leave space below each team name for scores and totals.

You also will have to manage the time allotted. Limit the total number of presenters, or drawers, to fifteen or less. For example, if thirty people are in the class and you have five groups of six people, have three members play from each group for a total of fifteen rounds. Each group must have the same number of presenters. Do not take longer than twenty minutes for the exercise.

Take out the three-by-five-inch index cards on which you have written phrases. The list of phrases goes from least to most difficult. Hand out the least difficult phrases first, and work up to the most difficult.

- Eye contact
- Speaking
- Power
- Silence
- Listening
- Nonverbal communication
- Conflict
- Message
- Gender
- Openness
- Culture
- Perception
- Friendship
- Empathy
- Gestures

Have the members of team 1 select who will draw first. Give this person an index card. He or she has one minute to draw and gesture while fellow team members guess the phrase.

 Facilitator: Provide a fresh flip-chart page for each drawing. When a team guesses correctly, give it 100 points on the second flip chart.

Continue the game with rounds of new artists from each team until the time is up and all teams have played an equal number of times. Recognize the winning team or teams.

Alternate option. You can give awards first to the winners and then to the other participants. Wrapped candies or chocolates make great awards.

Debrief the exercise. Ask, "What did you observe about communication during the game?" Other follow-up questions can include, What communication behaviors contributed to guessing the phrase? What role did expressiveness play in the group's success?

After participants have expressed their observations, remind them that they used verbal and nonverbal communication to solve the charade. Also, point out that the people who contributed the most when guessing and drawing communicated the most. They were the most expressive.

Training Tip: Managing Instructional Games

The purpose of the picture game is to involve the participants in experiential learning. This game should be fun; however, be aware that some people are competitive. Make sure everyone understands the rules, and monitor the game closely to ensure it runs smoothly. Clearly identify and reward the winning group (or groups). Be supportive and help all groups be successful.

Relationships

Time for segment: 35 minutes

> Relationships work according to principles. When we ignore these principles or violate them in some way, then we pay a price. When we understand the principles about how relationships work, we can be more productive and at ease with others.

 Facilitator: Display overheads 2.6 and 2.7, and review the principles of communication shown.

> *Principles of Communication*
>
> 1. Communication is two-way, not one-way.
> 2. All messages have content and relationship dimensions.
> 3. Relationships are either symmetrical or complementary.
>
> **2.6**

> *Principles of Communication (Cont.)*
>
> 4. You cannot *not* communicate
> 5. You cannot uncommunicate.
>
> **2.7**

You can study these principles at their source by reading the works of social scientist Gregory Bateson and the team of psychologists Paul Watzlawick, Janet Beavin, and Don Jackson.[3] Also, Joseph DeVito's *The Interpersonal Communcation Book* gives a good synopsis of these communication principles and respective examples.[4]

This section of the module uses lecture with overheads, questions, and interaction to impart the principles. Study the principles and find stories that make them come alive. The following is a synopsis of the five principles.

Principle #1. Communication is two-way, not one-way.

> The old view of communication was that all you had to do was design and deliver a great message, and that was all it took to be a great communicator. In the last century, those who studied communication came to understand that communication is transactional—that is, all parties in a conversation communicate continuously. An obvious exam-

ple is the nonverbal feedback a listener gives a speaker. A great skill to develop in communication is to observe how the listener is listening. In this classroom, while I am speaking, I am simultaneously listening to how well you listen and to gauge how much you are involved in our communication. Together we are interacting even though at this moment only one of us is speaking.

What is your sense of the listening in this room right now? Is your listening a message? Do you listen for how well others are listening to you when you speak? Do you ask people to listen to you when they appear not to?

Alternate option. An optional exercise is "listening for the listening." Have the participants form into pairs and speak for a couple of minutes each on a topic of interest. The speaker's objective, however, is to pay attention to how well the other person listens. After each partner gets a chance to speak, both partners give feedback to each other about how well they listened. The instructor then debriefs, asking, "How well did people listen? How well were you able to sense the other person's listening while you spoke?"

Principle 2. All messages have content and relationship dimensions.

When a manager sternly says to someone who reports to him or her, "I want to see you in my office immediately," this message's verbal, or *literal,* content is less important than what it says about the relationship. Can you imagine a middle manager in an organization walking up to the CEO and saying the same thing?

Facilitator: Display overhead 2.8, which explains the two levels of any message.

Content and Relationship Dimensions

Principle 2
Each message has two dimensions:
• Content—literal, or verbal
• Relationship—implicit, or nonverbal

2.8

Relationship messages tend to be nonverbal and implicit, or nonliteral. Notice, for instance, who starts and stops the conversation. Who signals the end of your business lunch simply by putting down his or her napkin and pushing back in the chair? Generally it is the person of higher status.

Principle 3. Relationships are either symmetrical or complementary.

Facilitator: Return to overheads 2.6 and 2.7.

Communication is not power neutral, and it pays to be aware of the power dimension of your relationships. In this sense we can classify any relationship as either symmetrical or complementary. In *symmetrical relationships,* partners share power equally. Both partners are equally assertive, aggressive, and passive. In *complementary relationships,* one member complements the other—for example, a passive person who looks for decisiveness in another joining with a powerful, decisive person.

Think of a symmetrical relationship you have at work. Now what about a complementary relationship? How about at home or in your personal relationships? Which type of relationship do you prefer?

Here you are trying to raise the participants' awareness of their relationship options. Participants need to understand these different kinds of relationships in their own lives. The point is not to judge, for seeking or ceding power and control is not necessarily negative. For example, the complementary relationship between Seiji Ozawa conducting and a great orchestra responding creates beautiful music.

Alternate option. DeVito's *The Interpersonal Communication Book* has exercises for identifying one-up, one-down, and one-across messages that are suitable for role plays.5 These exercises demonstrate the nature of symmetrical and complementary relationships and messages.

Principle 4. You cannot *not* communicate.

This principle is similar to the first—communication never stops. You cannot *not* communicate because communication is inevitable. Even if you do not respond to someone's communication, your lack of a response is still a message. Do you take longer to respond to some voice mail messages than others? Do you sometimes forget to respond altogether? What does your behavior say about the relationship?

 Facilitator: You can ask humorously here, "By the way, how long has it been since you called your mother?"

Principle 5. You cannot uncommunicate.

I have known people who have been fired from companies after sending e-mail messages that they later regretted sending. The lesson from their misfortune is you cannot uncommunicate: Be careful. Once a relationship message is sent, the effect is irreversible. Patching up afterward does not work nearly as well as sending the right message in the first place.

Another aspect of this inability to retract your messages is that every opportunity is unique at each moment of your life. The unique conditions you face at a particular moment will not exist again, ever—not in the same unique way. For example, if someone important to your career approaches you with an opportunity and you decline that offer, that particular opportunity under those particular conditions will never come again.

Can you personally recall any missed opportunities to develop a relationship with someone or to take advantage of an opportunity? The moral here is carpe diem, or seize the day.

Assertiveness

Time for segment: 10 minutes

Building on the foundation of listening and appreciation, assertiveness is key to effective interpersonal communication. In this section, you will explain the principles of assertiveness and work with particular assertiveness skills.

Assertiveness can be defined as speaking up for your rights, interests, and experience in a way that does not interfere with the rights and interests of others. Assertive individuals are open and direct. They stand up for their rights and interests without much anxiety, even when confronting an unpleasant situation.

 Facilitator: Display and read overhead 2.9.

> *Assertiveness, Passivity, and Aggressiveness*
>
> - *Assertiveness* is speaking up for your own rights and interests without violating the rights and interests of others.
> - *Passivity* is not speaking up for your own rights and interests.
> - *Aggressiveness* is acting for your own rights and interests in a way that violates the rights and interests of others.
>
> 2.9   © 2001 Joshua C. Garber

Assertiveness contrasts with both passivity and with aggressiveness. In *passive, or deferential behavior,* people do not stand up for their rights and interests. Such timid people accept what others tell them to do. Often nonassertive people even ask permission to do something that it is within their own rights.

Aggressive behavior occurs when people act in their own self-interest while violating the rights and interests of others. Some people are aggressive in almost any situation. Others are selective; they can be aggressive in some situations but not in others. One form of aggressiveness is *manipulation,* in which a person uses guilt and emotional appeals to get his or her way.

People often exhibit another common behavior, passive-aggressiveness, where they bottle up their resentments at having their rights violated and then one day just explode. In this event, the passive-aggressive person often thinks he or she is teaching the other person a lesson. The problem is, however, the other person rarely understands what the lesson is.

If someone asks you for a favor that is not in your best interest to perform, how would you respond? If you are passive, you might agree just to avoid the discomfort of saying no. If you are assertive, you might say, "Thanks for thinking of me, but I really do not have the time right now." If you are aggressive, you might say, "Forget it."

Facilitator: Display overhead 2.10.

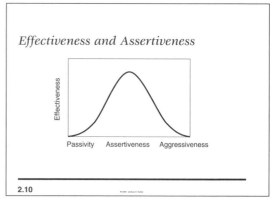

The graph in the overhead shows how effectiveness relates to assertiveness. The most effective people are assertive rather than passive or aggressive. Effectiveness increases as a person gains in assertiveness and then decreases as a person moves beyond assertiveness into aggressiveness.

Being assertive has definite benefits. Assertive people tend to:[6]

1. *Emerge as leaders in groups and organizations.* Others tend to support a person for a leadership role when that person speaks up for his own point of view, even if that point of view is contentious. However, others usually do not support the emergence of a leader who is aggressive, and passive people tend not to emerge as leaders.

2. *Establish and maintain productive interpersonal relationships.* Assertiveness washes away much of the uncertainty and confusion that undermine relationships.

3. *Overcome obstacles and get more of what they want.* By asserting their self-interests appropriately, assertive individuals ask more from life, and they get it.

4. *Uphold the rights, integrity, and dignity of self and others.* In saying what you mean and meaning what you say, communication becomes more honest and powerful.

5. *Experience greater job satisfaction.* Research supports the conclusion that assertive people enjoy their work more.

You might be interested to know that research also supports the conclusion that assertive individuals possess better dating skills. Assertive people who can describe what they want and need without raising the ire of others enjoy many benefits.

The principles of communication that we have just covered form a basis for understanding relationships. The next topic, appreciation, is the launching point for developing skills with assertiveness and your voice. Influence and voice for their own sake can be rather hollow, and besides, we would not have great influence if we did not start with an appreciation for others.

Appreciation

Time for segment: 30 minutes

Appreciating other people is a good place to begin in developing interpersonal relationships. *Appreciation* helps you understand the strengths and internal motivations of others. When you acknowledge their qualities and what drives them to succeed, you encourage other people to live courageously. Although it might seem paradoxical, appreciating other people enables us to influence them, also. The most powerful influence we can have on another human being is our ability to encourage that person to pursue his or her own inner direction. Further, this capacity to motivate others to work toward a common goal is a key to leadership.

Three steps are helpful in developing an appreciation of others. The first step is to appreciate yourself—to figure out your own strengths and what you want to achieve. Second, listen powerfully to others to determine their goals and strengths. Finally, respond to them in ways that encourage their commitment and action.

Exercise 2.2. Appreciating Self

The first part of the appreciation exercise is a personal visualization. As the term indicates, *interpersonal communication* is personal. To understand our relationships with others, first we have to understand ourselves.

As the instructor you must determine the format for visualization. If members know each other well and the setting is informal, you can do an elaborate visualization with people lying on their backs relaxing, listening to instrumental music, and concentrating on deep breathing. Participants in a residential, natural setting might go for this format. If you do ask people to lie on their backs, softly encourage them to stay completely flat and symmetrical, with their feet apart and hands at their sides.

In a more formal corporate setting, the visualization can take place with people sitting comfortably in chairs, closing their eyes, and taking a few deep breaths. The idea is to help people relax so they can find their source for rejuvenation. Ask participants to put down their pens, breathe deeply, and close their eyes. Work with them until they have comfortable, easy postures.

Here is an idea for a script to be read at a comfortable pace. You will want to change your script according to the nature of the situation.

> Begin by taking a few deep breaths. If you like, you can imagine yourself breathing in light—soft, warm light filling every pore and molecule of your body. As you breathe a natural, full breath, get in touch with your source of energy and renewal. Feel your body relax as you breathe. Feel your mind fill with light. Imagine your body becoming weightless.
>
> Feel the unique strengths within you—your unique self and wholeness. Imagine yourself accomplishing your goals, being successful, being able to make things happen with other people.
>
> Take a few more breaths. When you are ready, you can open your eyes and come back for our conversation.

You might want to debrief the visualization by asking the participants what their experience was like in the visualization. However, debriefing is not necessary. Remember, the purpose of the visualization was relaxation, renewal, and reflection.

Alternate option. If you do not want to lead a visualization with the group, you can prepare a handout. On the handout ask the participants to list their sources of strength and their motivations for accomplishment in life. Give them a few minutes to reflect and to complete the form.

Exercise 2.3. Appreciating Others

Listening is an integral part of interpersonal communication. Listening builds appreciation into a conversation. Next, you will work with a partner. You will each have an opportunity to speak and an opportunity to listen. When you speak, I would like you to share with the other person a deeply held goal, something close to your heart. The role of the listener is to encourage the speaker. Listeners, use your skills to be attentive and supportive. If necessary, ask questions that help the speakers clarify their goals. Your aim is to help the speakers rally their enthusiasm in pursuit of their goals. Assure them that their goals are worthwhile and that they can accomplish them.
Remember:

- Give the speakers your total attention and time.
- Stay focused on their topic.
- Use the speakers' names in your responses.
- Try to understand their perspective.
- Avoid responding with your own stories.
- Do not finish their sentences for them.
- Identify their strengths and assets.
- Encourage them to pursue their goals and be successful.

Give the speakers three minutes, and then tell them to change roles. After the exercise, it is not necessary to debrief. However, if you sense the participants want to discuss their experience, help them out. Let them talk.

 Facilitator: The three activities in this segment gain in momentum. Next is the slippery egg relay!

Exercise 2.4. The Slippery Egg Relay

Use a method such as counting off to assign people to teams of four or five people each. Next, everyone helps rearrange the room so that the center of the room is clear. Move the tables out of the way. Then for each team set up a row of chairs about twenty feet long with the chairs spaced about four feet apart in the rows. In the relay, each team member takes a turn threading between the chairs in the row—on the left and right alternately. Each person weaves all the way along the row and then back, where the slippery egg is handed off to the next person. The goal of the slippery egg relay is to be the first team to have every member get the oil-coated egg down the course and back.

 Facilitator: Display overheads 2.11 and 2.12, and explain the relay's rules.

Rules for the Slippery Egg Relay
• Each team has two spoons—one for the runner and the other for the next runner.
• Each team member runs the entire course with an egg on a spoon.
• Only the spoon can touch the egg. If anything else touches the egg, you must start over.

2.11

You need at least two teaspoons and two oil-coated eggs for each team. The extra egg is in case someone on the team drops the egg, and it breaks.

 Facilitator: Encourage the teams to cheer for each other. "Show me enthusiasm!"

Rules for the Slippery Egg Relay (Cont.)
• The egg must stay on the spoon.
• When team members complete the course, they must transfer the egg using only the spoons. No hands!
• You must cheer your teammates.
• The first team to have all members finish and sit down wins!

2.12

Rearrange the room after the game so people can sit down. When the room is back together, debrief the exercise. Ask the participants, "Did encouragement help? What did it feel like to encourage others? What did it feel like to be encouraged?" Steer the discussion toward the idea that a key factor in building winning relationships and teams is to be able to appreciate and encourage others. Appreciation builds a strong foundation for assertiveness, which together result in trust.

Asking

Time for segment: 35 minutes

> The next assertiveness skill we will work with is asking for what you want. In their book *The Aladdin Factor,* Jack Canfield and Mark Hansen wrote that many people lead unfulfilled lives because they do not ask for what they want.[7] We are afraid to ask or feel we are not worthy. We overestimate the obstacles, and we do not appreciate the potential value of obstacles as incentives.

 TRAINING TIP: ASK FOR WHAT YOU WANT

To underscore the promise of asking for what you want, you can tell stories about things you have asked for and received. You can find many such stories in *The Aladdin Factor.* Also, this segment is an opportunity for you, the trainer, to ask for what you want. You can ask the participants to do something humorous like get up on their feet and give you a standing ovation. Whatever you ask the trainees to do, relate it back to the idea that they can get what they want, but first they have to ask for it.

> Before we ask for anything, first we should figure out exactly what we want. So the first step in asking is prioritizing what we want. Prioritization is an essential skill in assertiveness. Why assert yourself for something that is not important?
>
> Turn to activity 2.1 in your workbook, and take a few minutes to write down your wishes. In the first list brainstorm what you want at work—more respect, a corner office, promotion to CEO—and write it down. The second list is what you want in your personal, family, and social lives. List anything you truly desire—love, harmony, friends, saving the world.

Give the participants four minutes to complete their lists. Monitor their work to check for progress and questions.

Next, the participants select something from their personal or professional lives they could ask for. Then they brainstorm a list of reasons why asking for what they want is difficult.

 Facilitator: Read out loud the workbook activity instructions.

 Facilitator: Prepare a flip chart to record the participants' reasons.

After the participants finish steps 1 and 2, ask them for some of their reasons why asking for something is difficult. Record these on a flip chart.

After you record the list, analyze their responses. Most probably have to do with fear, with a lack of belief in the generosity of others, and with not feeling worthy enough. Encourage the participants to overcome these limitations in their thinking and to take a risk and ask for something.

 Facilitator: Display and read the inspirational quotes on overheads 2.13 and 2.14.

Asking Quotes

- You miss 100 percent of the shots you do not take.
  —Wayne Gretsky
- If you don't ask, you don't get.
  —Mohandas Gandhi
- Never, never, never, never give up.
  —Winston Churchill

2.13

Asking Quotes (Cont.)

- We tend to get what we expect.
  —Norman Vincent Peale
- You must do the thing you think you cannot do.
  —Eleanor Roosevelt

2.14

KNOWING WHAT YOU WANT

A key to effective assertiveness is knowing *when* to be assertive. Being assertive takes time and energy, and we need focus. One way to be effective is to prioritize. Why be assertive about things you do not care about? Save your assertiveness and focus it on things that are important to you. Know your interests.

Step 1. What You Want in Your Work and Professional Life

In the box below, write down the things that you want in your work and professional life.

What you want at work and professionally:

_____

_____

_____

_____

_____

_____

_____

_____

_____

_____

_____

_____

_____

_____

_____

Step 2. What You Want in Your Personal Life

Next, make a list of things that you want in your personal, family, and social life. Brainstorm. These aspirations can be emotional, relational, material, or spiritual.

What you want in your personal life:

_____

_____

_____

_____

_____

_____

_____

_____

_____

_____

_____

_____

_____

_____

_____

_____

_____

_____

Remember what you want. Your priorities mark the important conversations where assertiveness belongs.

Ask the participants to turn to workbook activity 2.2, and talk them through step 3. Review the tips to the art of asking:

- Be direct and specific.
- Ask with the expectation of success.
- Ask someone who has the power to give you whatever you want.
- Use humor.
- Ask a higher power.
- Ask with conviction and purpose.
- Ask again.

Pepper this segment with stories that fill the participants' imaginations with ideas about asking. For example, think of someone you know who asked for a promotion, raise, new project, or job, and got it. Asking is a crucial skill in assertiveness. Like many assertiveness skills, asking for something depends on our self-confidence.

 Facilitator: Complete and debrief step 3 in workbook activity 2.2.

Midpoint Break

Time for break: 15 minutes

Clearly state your expectations about the participants returning on time. After the break you will cover the topics of self-confidence and advocacy.

Self-Confidence

Time for segment: 40 minutes

In defining assertiveness, we include self-confident behavior. A major obstacle to assertiveness and to asking for what you want is the lack of self-confidence. Deep inside most of us is at least a seed of doubt about our worthiness. Some of us even feel we are not worthy of our wish-list items from the last exercise. We fear the personal and external obstacles are insurmountable.

Instead of using this faulty reasoning, however, we should assume the best. Remember, the optimist risks failure while the pessimist avoids success. So take your pick, and pick wisely. As Johann Wolfgang Goethe said, "Whatever you can do, or dream you can, begin it. Boldness has genius, power, and magic in it."

Assertiveness is about the bold realm of possibility, which is much better than we can imagine for it is endless. It all begins right here, with self-confidence, and self-confidence determines how we handle that self-generated obstacle to assertiveness—fear. With effort and insight, we can build our self-confidence, overcome our fears, and get what we want out of life.

ASKING FOR WHAT YOU WANT

In this activity, you prepare to ask for what you want. Review the two lists you wrote in activity 2.1.

Step 1. Selecting

Select something you want to ask for from your professional or personal lists.

Something you would like to ask for:

_____

_____

_____

_____

_____

_____

Step 2. Why Asking Is Difficult

Next, consider the reasons why asking for this item (or receiving it) could be difficult. Write your reasons in the space below.

Reasons why asking for this item is difficult:

_____

_____

_____

_____

_____

_____

_____

Step 3. Ask for It

In the box below record (1) what you will ask for, (2) who you will ask, and (3) how you will ask for it.

Remember these guidelines for asking:

- Be direct and specific.
- Ask with the expectation of success.
- Ask someone who has the power to give you what you want.
- Use humor.
- Ask a higher power.
- Ask with conviction and purpose.
- Ask again.

What you will ask for:

_____

_____

_____

_____

_____

Who you will ask:

_____

How you will ask for it:

_____

_____

_____

_____

_____

_____

_____

Facilitator: Display and read the quotes on overheads 2.15 through 2.17.

Today, being self-confident and assertive are more important than ever before. In our competitive world pounding with change and information overload, how do we get others' attention and get our message through? For others to hear us first we must develop strong voices. For others to recognize us we must promote our strengths. Finally, for our own success, we must first believe in ourselves and our self-worth.

Facilitator: Direct the participants' attention to activity 2.3 in their workbooks.

In this exercise, the participants make three lists:

1. My accomplishments so far in life

2. What others like about me

3. My strengths, what I do well

Assertiveness Quotes

- Feel the fear and do it anyway.

  —Susan Jeffers
- All things are difficult before they are easy.

  —Thomas Fuller

2.15

Assertiveness Quotes (Cont.)

- Most of the important things in the world have been accomplished by people who have kept on trying when there seemed to be no hope at all.

  —Dale Carnegie

2.16

Assertiveness Quotes (Cont.)

- All that is necessary to break the spell of inertia and frustration is this: Act as if it were impossible to fail. That is the talisman, the formula, the command of right-about-face which turns us from failure towards success.

  —Dorothea Brande

2.17

Facilitator: Tell the participants that now is the time to brag!

They do not need to show anyone else these lists, although you will ask them to share a couple of items later. Ask them to brainstorm the possibilities and to write down the first thing that comes to mind. Remind them to work with their strengths.

Check in with the participants to see if they need help. Ask everyone to write at least three items for each list. Cajole them, if necessary: "Yes, come on, each of us has things that we're proud of." For the second list—what others like about you—ask them to search their memory for every compliment they have ever received. Write them down.

YOUR STRENGTHS AND ACCOMPLISHMENTS

Another tool for developing self-confidence is working with your strengths and accomplishments. Although we can shore up our weaknesses, this work is seldom as gratifying and productive as leading with our strengths.

Step 1. Your Accomplishments

In the space below, write down your major accomplishments.

Your accomplishments thus far in life:

Step 2. What People Like about You

Next, write down what people like about you. Prod your memory for compliments. Believe them.

What others like about you:

_____

_____

_____

_____

_____

_____

_____

_____

_____

_____

_____

_____

_____

_____

_____

_____

_____

_____

_____

_____

_____

Step 3. Your Strengths

Next list your strengths. Brainstorm a list of what you do well.

Your strengths:

_____

_____

_____

_____

_____

_____

_____

_____

_____

_____

_____

_____

_____

_____

_____

_____

_____

_____

Remember your accomplishments, the compliments you've received, and your strengths. Build on them to accomplish even more.

Debrief after they all have at least three items in each list. Ask them to turn to a partner and share at least one item from each list. Give them each two minutes to share. Remind them of the time at halftime.

Alternate option. You can do this exercise with the whole group. Go around the room and have each person explain one item from each list.

After the workbook activity, remind the participants that it is important for their success and for their self-confidence to work with their strengths. Self-worth is something we can build. Positive interpersonal relationships begin with positive self-regard. When we think positively about ourselves, we project self-confidence and others respond to us accordingly.

 Facilitator: Tell a story about what self-confidence and self-promotion have done for someone.

In this time of information overload, self-promotion is necessary just to get noticed. We can take a lesson on self-promotion from history—from Thomas Edison, for example. Contrary to popular belief, he was not the first person to invent the lightbulb. Sir Humphry Davy, an English chemist, produced arc-light illumination as early as 1802, and two other Europeans demonstrated the lightbulb successfully before Edison. But Thomas Edison knew how to promote himself and was able to sell his invention commercially; hence he became known as the inventor of the lightbulb.

In the next segment, we will explore ways to project self-confidence with our speech.

Vocal Self-Confidence

A key to learning self-confidence is to act confidently. A place to start is with the voice, which is the nonverbal dimension to speaking. According to the principles of interpersonal communication we discussed earlier in this session, all messages have content and relationship dimensions. Although our use of language has a literal, or content, dimension and this dimension is important, the quality of our voice sends a powerful message about the relationship.

For example, many misunderstandings do not come from what we say literally. They stem instead from our tone of voice, which can change the meaning of what we say. Here is an example. When you say to someone, "Thanks a lot." with a sincere intonation, you mean you indeed are thankful. Use a sarcastic tone, however, and you mean "stop doing that."

How many of you have worked with your voice in theater, public speaking, or choral music? If you have worked with your voice, then you are aware that your voice itself has great influence, and you can knowingly use your voice to accomplish certain purposes. You can talk your child to sleep after a nightmare, for example, or you can power-fully make a point at a meeting and get people to listen to you.

Training Tip: Working with Voice

Here again, you must adapt your instruction to the trainees. The exercise that follows involves a form of self-expression that some people might not be comfortable with. Some groups enjoy doing unusual activities. They like being instructed to *roar* like a lion at the top of their lungs. Other groups might be too inhibited, though. Use your best judgment about your group, and proceed accordingly.

Exercise 2.5. Vocal Power

One great way to develop your voice is to join a choir. Have you ever noticed the extraordinary voices of actors and professional singers? As with other skills, you can develop your voice. François de la Rochefoucauld once said about the art of conversation, "There is no less eloquence in the tone of the voice, in the eyes and in the air of a speaker, than in his choice of words."[8]

Ask the participants to stand up and move into a circle or a U-shape. Pull tables or chairs out of the way, if necessary. They need room.

First, stand comfortably. Find your center of gravity. Do not have anything in your hands. Maybe you'd feel good standing with your feet shoulder-width apart. Let your hands fall normally by your sides. We will begin with breathing. As all singers know, developing our voices begins with learning proper breathing.

Place your hand over your diaphragm, at the top of your belly where your rib cage divides. Through your nose, take a deep breath from your diaphragm. The diaphragm maintains your tone as you speak. Take another deep breath. Feel the diaphragm rise first and then, in sequence, your lower, middle, and upper lungs. At the end of your inhalation, feel your collarbone rise. Now exhale fully. Repeat the deep breathing until it feels natural. Focus on feeling your diaphragm contract and expand.

The vocal chords in your larynx produce sound. As you exhale air over these chords, they vibrate and—voilà!—sound. Keep breathing. Now sound out the days of the week—Monday, Tuesday, Wednesday . . . — with each becoming more powerful until you say the word *Sunday!* Feel each syllable, each sound. Enunciate. Do it again.

Next, we will practice a lower, more powerful voice. Go lower in tone. Think about the deep voices of Samuel L. Jackson, Kristen Johnson (*Third Rock from the Sun*), James Earl Jones, or Kathleen Turner. Repeat after me, and let's make our voices mimic our words: "I can speak lower and lower and lower." Again: "I can speak lower and lower and lower."

We are also powerful when we speak louder. Research demonstrates that higher-status people tend to speak louder than lower-status people. So let's say, "I can speak louder and louder and louder." Repeat.

 Facilitator: Prepare a flip-chart page with the phrases below.

Now, let's recite together each of these phrases—and don't forget to roar!

- I am powerful when I speak lower.
- I am powerful when I speak louder.
- And when I speak lower and louder, I *r-o-a-r!*

Everybody ought to shake when they roar.

You can continue to play sound games. Another variation is with vowels. Ask the participants to make the "oo" sound from their gut, the "ah" sound from the center of their chests, and the "ee" sound from their heads just above the mouth cavity. You can also work with the "mm" sound from the top of their heads. Another variation is to practice reading some text, such as a play or a quote, out loud. The objective is to add power by experimenting with the tone, pitch, timbre, pace, resonance, and volume of their voices.

When you are finished, ask the participants to sit down. Encourage them to develop their voices—to join a choir, take acting lessons, or use feedback from audio recorders.

Self-Talk

This section covers another aspect of assertiveness—self-talk. *Self-talk* is the private conversation each of us carries on inside our heads. Our inner dialogue is a source of tremendous power. The secret to self-confidence and to assertiveness is being positive.

Here are some examples of positive self-talk.

- I can do this.
- Today is a great day.
- I am happy.
- Success is mine.
- I am enthusiastic.

With positive self-talk you can build your enthusiasm and energy as well as your self-confidence. Whenever you feel negative, give yourself a boost with positive, motivating self-talk.

Training Tip: Self-Talk

Here again use your best judgment to fit the needs of your group. You have the option of practicing self-talk with the participants. For example, you can take one of the phrases listed above and repeat it with the group. Dale Carnegie used the phrase, "*Act* enthusiastic and you will *be* enthusiastic." I knew a long-distance runner who used to push himself by repeating over and over, "Eat my dust." Ask the participants if they have any self-talk phrases to offer.

Advocacy

Time for segment: 40 minutes

Advocacy builds on the features of assertiveness we have already discussed—relationships, appreciation, asking, and self-confidence. *Advocacy* means taking a stand for something you believe in and making declarations intended to change others' attitudes. Our first topic in the study of advocacy is powerful language.

Powerful Language

Just like the ways in which we use our voices suggest power, literal language has great power, also. Some words and phrases are weak; others are strong. We should choose our words carefully to give our messages greater impact. For instance, when we want to be tentative, we should tone down our speech. However, we want to be aware when we do this. Often, people speak tentatively when more powerful speech would serve their purpose better. Next, we will practice using powerful speech.

Facilitator: Display and read overheads 2.18 and 2.19. Leave the overheads up for participants to see during the next exercise.

Exercise 2.6. Powerful Speech

In this exercise, the trainees practice using powerful speech while identifying a controversy at work.

A *controversy* is an issue that has two sides or two arguments. Society is filled with controversies, for example, gun control, speed limits, English-only public schools.

Powerful and Powerless Speech

Powerful	*Powerless*
• No qualifiers—"All men are created equal."	• Qualifiers—"I think that all men are created equal."
• No verbal pauses	• Verbal pauses—"ah, er, um, uh, and . . ."

2.18

Powerful and Powerless Speech (Cont.)

Powerful	*Powerless*
• Declarative language— "When profits rise . . ."	• Hedges—"Don't get me wrong but . . ."
• Positive attitude— "I will be happy to."	• Negative attitude—"Only if I have to . . ."

2.19

TAKING A STAND

The purpose of this activity is to practice the skills for taking a stand on a controversial topic—a controversy either at work or in society.

Step 1. Brainstorm and Select a Controversy

In the space below, brainstorm ideas for a controversy you could discuss. Any idea is a good idea. After you make your list, circle one controversy you will address.

Controversies (brainstorm many, circle one):

_____

_____

_____

_____

_____

_____

_____

_____

_____

_____

_____

_____

_____

_____

_____

_____

_____

Step 2. Use Powerful Language

In the next box, practice using powerful language for the controversy you wish to address. Using the guidelines for powerful speech, write a paragraph.

Write your argument using powerful language:

Facilitator: Ask trainees to turn to workbook activity 2.4.

The first step in the workbook activity is to pick a controversy either at work or in society. Next, pick the side of the controversy you will advocate. Everyone picks their own controversy. Next, write a paragraph describing your argument. Refer to the overhead for guidelines on powerful speech. Use this exercise to practice eliminating powerless language.

Give the participants about four minutes to write out their arguments. Check in with those who appear to have difficulty. Help them identify a controversy, their stand on the issue, and their argument.

Divide the class into pairs and instruct them to take turns voicing their arguments. Ask them to use the features of powerful speech and to eliminate the forms of powerless speech.

Each person will probably have a unique controversy. This result is not a problem because the exercise is not really an interaction. It is an opportunity for each person to use powerful speech in a difficult situation—a controversy.

The first speaker gets two and a half minutes to present his arguments. The listeners are not to agree or disagree. They only listen. Ask the pairs to debrief. Then ask the questions, "How well did the speakers conform to the features of powerful speech? Did they use any powerless speech forms?" Then reverse the roles, and the second person speaks. Debrief again, using the same questions. Don't forget to debrief the group as a whole.

How difficult was it to use powerful language when arguing a controversy? What made it difficult? What would you do differently? At what times would you want to use powerless speech? There are times when we might want to be tentative—when we are arguing with an inflexible boss, for example—however, we need to know how to speak powerfully. We need to know the differences between powerful and powerless speech and how to use the different forms appropriately.

Intervening in conversations

Intervening in conversations is an advanced communication skill. Examples of interventions are:

- Asking someone to listen when they are not
- Regaining control after someone interrupts you
- Asking for respect when someone is disrespectful

Facilitator: Display and read overheads 2.20 and 2.21, which summarize how to intervene in a conversation.

An intervention consists of three steps. The first step is deciding whether or not to intervene. Here, return to your priorities. What do you want? If the relationship or issue is unimportant, why bother? Intervene when the conversation concerns something or someone important to you.

The second step is giving feedback, or stating in direct language what was publicly observable about the other person's behavior. For example, when someone interrupts you, say, "Just a moment, please, you began speaking before I finished my sentence." The third step is asking for what you want. In keeping with the last example, you finish with "I would like to finish my explanation and then hear your response to it."

Intervening in Conversations

- Intervene when the listener:
  - Does not listen
  - Cuts you off
  - Is disrespectful
- Step 1. Decide whether to intervene.
  - Is the relationship important?
  - Does the behavior affect something important to you, a priority?

2.20

Intervening in Conversations (Cont.)

- Step 2. Give feedback.
  - State what was publicly observable about the person's behavior.
    - For example, "Just a moment, you began speaking before I finished my sentence."
  - Avoid being judgmental.
- Step 3. Ask for what you want.
  - "Please listen while I finish."

2.21

 Facilitator: Leave overheads displayed as you introduce the next activity.

The workbook activity gives the participants a chance to work through an example intervention. First, read out loud the case detailed on the worksheets. Then, instruct them to work through the three steps. Give them five minutes to complete the written work.

After they finish, debrief using the model. Was it time to intervene? How did they respond? Did they do step 2 and feed back Terry's actual words? Did they do step 3 and ask directly for what they wanted?

Exercise 2.7. Intervention Role-Play

In this role-play, two participants act out the roles in the case study in workbook activity 2.5. Ask for two volunteers whose plans intervene in this situation. If no one volunteers, then ask two people who you believe would be good actors to play Terry and the interventionist. We will call the interventionist Chris. Give clear instructions for the role-play. Instruct (1) Chris to follow the

INTERVENING IN CONVERSATIONS

The purpose of this activity is to practice the three steps for intervening in a conversation. Read the following case. Then describe how you would respond.

You have decided to become more assertive. You feel that one person in particular, Terry, does not respect you in conversations. You have decided to intervene the next time he is disrespectful.

You and Terry are peers in a purchasing department, but he frequently makes "one-up" comments. You and Terry are in a room alone discussing a particular purchase. After you propose researching some alternate vendors for this purchase, Terry says seriously, "What do *you* know?"

In the space below, use the steps for intervening in conversations and describe how you would respond to Terry.

Your response:

_____

_____

_____

_____

_____

_____

_____

_____

_____

_____

_____

_____

_____

guidelines, (2) Terri to respond favorably to Chris's intervention, and (3) Terry to come around and be more respectful of Chris. Get the group's full attention for the performance. If the "volunteer" playing either role—Chris or Terri—is not successful, give that person a chance to fix the performance and try again. It is important that the role-plays are successful for the participants. Coach them until they do succeed. Finally, debrief the exercise. Include the actors by asking them what they felt worked and did not work in the intervention. How was the role-play for them? What did they learn? Then, ask the rest of the group for their impressions.

Powerful language—what if you mess up?

So far in our study of assertiveness, we have been asking others for such things as respect but what do we do when we assert ourselves and then mess up? When we make a mistake or upset someone, our recourse is quite simple: Admit it and keep moving. Do not beat yourself up with excessive apologies and self-denigration. In some cases, it is a good idea to apologize and make amends. In most cases, though, it is enough to smile and admit your mistake.

Make sure you learn from your mistakes, but keep moving. The true test of your self-confidence is how you respond when you mess up or when you are under attack.

A great story about standing up to an attack comes from former President Ronald Reagan.

 Facilitator: In order to make this story uplifting, tell it with appreciation for President Reagan's confidence in the face of adversity.

In 1982, during his second term in office, Reagan's approval rating from the American people was the lowest for a second-term president in U.S. history. Only one year before, when he was shot by a would-be assassin, Reagan's popularity had reached an all-time high. When President Reagan heard about his low ratings from his pollster, he said with a smile, "Don't worry, I'll just go out and get myself shot again." Reagan's response was a good example of self-confidence in the face of adversity.

Nonverbal assertiveness

Our discussion of assertiveness would not be complete without covering nonverbal assertiveness. We first addressed this element in our exercise with voice. The quality of our voice, or *paralanguage,* is a form of nonverbal communication. Remember that every message has two levels—both content and relationship—with the relationship message being nonverbal. As retired Colonel Gene Harrison, a professional speaker, once said, "You are the message."[9]

In addition to our voice, we express nonverbal assertiveness through our appearance, that is, our body, our style of clothing and hair, our use of personal space, our artifacts such as office decorations and cars, our facial expressions and posture, how we manage time, and how we move. Like all messages, these messages can be powerful or weak. Be attuned to your nonverbal communication so that you convey the right message.

 Facilitator: Display overheads 2.22 and 2.23.

 Training Tip: Nonverbal Communication

Stories, examples, and role plays are quite useful in teaching nonverbal communication. For each of the items on overheads 2.22 and 2.23, prepare an illustrative story or an example. If you feel it is appropriate, you can use people in the class as examples. Point out persons in the class who are dressed professionally, use engaging facial expressions, or have great posture. Give compliments as appropriate. Examples of nonverbal communication can easily be humorous and engaging. From television sitcoms like *Seinfeld* you

Nonverbal Assertiveness

- Appearance
- Space
- Voice
- Environment
- Facial expressions
- Posture
- Time

2.22

Nonverbal Assertiveness (Cont.)

- Movement:
  - Walk with an even stride.
  - Swing arms a little.
  - Keep head up.
  - Take in surroundings.
  - Glance carefully at others.
  - Walk briskly.

2.23

can pull interesting stories and comedy about interpersonal communication. Also, DeVito's *The Interpersonal Communication Book* has useful chapters on nonverbal communication.[10]

 Facilitator: Put overhead 2.22 back up.

Here is sample background material for each of the items on overheads 2.22 and 2.23.

1. The first nonverbal category is your appearance, which consists of your clothing and body. Consider your wardrobe and your hairstyle. Update them both, and dress for success. Do you work out? Your physical body sends a message, also. Research concludes that organizations are more likely to hire or promote tall and good-looking people. Maybe it is unfair, but we can do a great deal to improve or enhance our appearance.

2. Next is how we use space. The personal space we occupy varies with status and cultural norms. High-status people seem to take up more personal space, which for most Americans extends about eighteen

inches from our bodies. The social space in which we like to carry on conversations is even greater, or between eighteen inches and four feet—but in Arab and Hispanic cultures, personal and social spaces are much smaller. An Arab could consider an American rude for wanting to carry on a conversation while standing four feet apart.

3. We have already studied the tone of our voice as a message. Also consider its quality. Unpleasant voices detract from communication while a beautiful, soothing voice is like a siren's song—it calls us and draws us in.

4. Now think about your environment, including your car, and how you decorate and take care of your space. If you want the corner office, fix up the space you have now, and start working toward a better space.

5. Facial expressions communicate your entire range of emotion and activity from alertness and interest to turn-taking in conversations. Your expression not only influences your audience, it can affect how you feel as well. Right now try a broadcasters' technique: Sit up straight, keep your hands free of objects, lick your lips, open your mouth wide, and *smile* broadly. Don't you feel different now? Research has proven that smiling changes how you feel. Remember, act enthusiastic, and you will be enthusiastic.

6. Your posture communicates your emotions and your relationships to others. Look at yourself right now. Are you leaning forward in anticipation or slouching from boredom?

7. The way you manage time sends others a message. Do you show up on time? Do others? Do you return phone calls? How long does it take? Consider what these behaviors tell other people. As with personal space, the use of time also varies by culture. Americans tend to be literal with time while Africans and Hispanics tend to have greater tolerance for starting meetings after the specified start time.

 Facilitator: Switch to overhead 2.23.

8. Your range of motion also conveys your attitude and energy. For example, you communicate confidence when you walk with an even stride, keep your head up, swing your arms, and swagger just a little.

So far in this segment, we have covered many elements of assertiveness—knowing what we want, self-confidence, powerful language, and nonverbal assertiveness. Next, we will move to the topic of advocacy.

The PRES model for advocacy

Have you ever advocated something at a meeting and your words fell into dead air? Did it seem as if no one even listened, or that there was no energy in the room? Most of us have had that experience at least once. In this segment we are going to work with a method for being persuasive with ideas. This method, called the PRES model, builds on everything we have done up to now in the workshop.

Advocacy is important in conversations, in leadership, and in professional development. Research has proven the ability to persuade others is a key characteristic of successful executives. Although we need to be powerful listeners, our conversations are not fulfilled only by listening; we must use strong expression, or the ability to impact our world with our ideas.

Facilitator: Display and introduce overheads 2.24 and 2.25. Explain the four steps and give the example.

Facilitator: Prepare at least one good story about how a particular advocacy was a breakthrough for a person or a community.

> **The PRES Advocacy Model**
>
> • *Point*
>   • The proposed flextime system will serve the best interests of the organization.
> • *Reason*
>   • According to our HR analysis, we need to attract and attain the most talented people, and we need high morale in the face of our challenges.
>   • The flextime system will be a lure to attract talent, and it will be a benefit to keep and motivate the talent we have, all without adding cost.
>
> 2.24

> **The PRES Advocacy Model (Cont.)**
>
> • *Example*
>   • Two other business units in our company added flextime systems, and their attrition rates fell significantly.
> • *Summary*
>   • The best decision is to adopt the flextime system.
>
> 2.25

We now will work through an example of the PRES model. Turn to workbook activity 2.6.

Before you begin writing, identify a position you want to advocate. This issue can be anything at work, from a strategic direction for your company to a policy regarding the use of office supplies. Take a moment to brainstorm the issues you want to address.

Next, pick an advocacy you want to work with. You will practice it and refine it, and then some of you will present your advocacy to the group. Use all of the skills, or competencies, for assertiveness, both verbal and nonverbal.

In your workbooks, you have space to work on each step of your advocacy. Write down your argument one step at a time—your point, your reasons, an example, and a summary. I will check in with you in five minutes.

Check in with the participants and see if they need help. When they are finished, direct their attention to the next exercise.

PREPARING FOR ADVOCACY

In this activity, you will use the PRES advocacy model. First of all, determine an advocacy you wish to make. This issue can be anything at work, from a strategic direction for your company to a policy regarding the use of office supplies.

Step 1. State Your Point

Clearly make your point.

Point:

_____

_____

_____

_____

_____

_____

_____

_____

_____

_____

_____

_____

_____

_____

_____

_____

Step 2. Give Your Reason

Provide the reason(s) you make this claim. Reason is evidence logically related to your point. Therefore, provide evidence and be logical.

Reason:

Step 3. Give an Example

Where has this idea worked before? Give an example.

Example:

Step 4. Summarize

Finally, give a brief summary of your advocacy.

Summary:

_____

_____

_____

_____

_____

_____

_____

_____

_____

_____

_____

_____

_____

_____

_____

_____

_____

_____

_____

_____

_____

_____

_____

_____

_____

_____

Exercise 2.8. Practicing with a Partner

In this exercise, the participants practice with a partner and get some feedback to refine their advocacy. Here are the steps:

1. Form trainees into pairs.
2. Let the partners decide who speaks first.
3. The first partner advocates while the other listens.
4. Partners debrief: Did they use the PRES model, powerful language, and assertive nonverbal communication?
5. The first partner takes some time to revise his or her advocacy.
6. Partners change roles and repeat the process.

Debrief the group as a whole. What did they learn using the PRES model?

Exercise 2.9. Practicing in Front of the Group

If you have the time, let everyone have a turn. Fewer participants can speak if the group is too large or time does not permit. Adjust your instructions accordingly.

I would like you to come to the front of the group and demonstrate your models. Who wants to go first?

 Training Tip: Calling on Participants

As the instructor it is your job to get people involved. At first, determine who wants to speak and let them. However, you need to get everyone involved. Call on quiet people. Use reason to encourage them to speak: "We just spent a few hours exploring assertiveness, and now is the time to grab the bull by the horns. Who have we not heard from?" Also, call on people by name. Be friendly and inviting. Expect participation, but don't compel people to speak in front of the group.

Debrief. Ask the presenter about his or her experience. Ask the rest of the class their opinions, too. In a supportive atmosphere, coach each person to do his or her best. When enough people have presented their models, summarize the four steps in the PRES advocacy model.

SUMMARY

Time for segment: 30 minutes

Now it is time to reflect on our development in assertiveness. In this session, we have explored skills for interpersonal assertiveness and influence, examined powerful language and the nature of self-confidence, and worked with advocacy. Now we want to summarize our experiences and determine what we each want to develop related to assertiveness.

The development plan for assertiveness follows the same steps as the development plan in module 1.

 Facilitator: Display and read overhead 2.26, and quickly summarize the steps again.

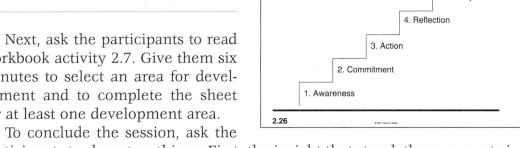

Next, ask the participants to read workbook activity 2.7. Give them six minutes to select an area for development and to complete the sheet for at least one development area.

To conclude the session, ask the participants to share two things: First, the insight that struck them as most significant in the session and second, their development area.

After the participants have contributed their thoughts, end the session powerfully. Encourage the participants to take what they learned into their work and personal lives.

Life is about our relationships with other people. Assertiveness and authenticity are key dimensions of healthy relationships. At the end of our lives, we will not regret the risks we took and the mistakes we made. Rather, we will regret the risks and assertions we failed to make.

NOTES

1. S. C. Harper, "Business Education: A View from the Top," *Business Forum* 12 (summer 1987).
2. S. P. Morreale, M. M. Osborn, and J. Pearson, "Why Communication Is Important: An Argument Supporting the Centrality of the Communication Discipline," *Journal of the Association of Communication Administrators,* November 1999.
3. G. Bateson, *Steps to an Ecology of Mind* (Chicago: University of Chicago Press, 2000), and P. Watzlawick, J. H. Beavin, and D. D. Jackson, *Pragmatics of Human Communication: A Study of Interactional Patterns, Pathologies, and Paradoxes* (New York: W. W. Norton, 1967).
4. J. A. DeVito, *The Interpersonal Communication Book,* 8th ed. (Reading, MA: Addison-Wesley, 1997).
5. DeVito, *The Interpersonal Communication Book.*
6. J. Davidson, *The Complete Idiot's Guide to Assertiveness* (New York: Macmillan, 1997), and DeVito, *The Interpersonal Communication Book.*
7. J. Canfield and M. V. Hansen, *The Aladdin Factor* (New York: Berkley, 1995).
8. Dale Carnegie. *Public Speaking and Influencing Men in Business* (New York: Association Press, 1951) p. 120.
9. Lily Walters, *Secrets of Successful Speakers: How You Can Motivate, Captivate, and Persuade* (New York: McGraw-Hill 1993), p. 101.
10. DeVito, *The Interpersonal Communication Book.*

DEVELOPMENT PLAN FOR ASSERTIVENESS

Reflect on the skills and attitudes you have studied in this session. Answer the question, "What assertiveness skill or attitude would be a breakthrough for me?" We are working with the first step in the development process—awareness. Brainstorm answers in the space below. All possibilities are good possibilities.

Possible development areas:

_____

_____

_____

_____

_____

_____

_____

_____

_____

_____

Next select an area for development. Consider the following criteria.

- The development goal should be a *breakthrough* for you in your relationships with others.
- The goal is *concrete*—that is, you and others can observe whether you perform the behavior.
- The *results* of the goal are observable. For example, if you perform the behavior well, you will observe its positive effects in others and in your relationships.
- You select the goal freely and feel an *internal commitment* toward this goal.

Write your goal on the following form.

Development Area 1

Your commitment to development in assertiveness:

_____

_____

_____

_____

Why you have selected this goal:

_____

_____

_____

_____

How you will accomplish this goal (include research, plans, behaviors):

_____

_____

_____

_____

Others who can help you accomplish this goal:

_____

_____

_____

How you will follow up and know if you are successful:

_____

_____

_____

_____

Development Area 2

Your commitment to development in assertiveness:

_____

_____

_____

_____

_____

Why you have selected this goal:

_____

_____

_____

_____

_____

How you will accomplish this goal (include research, plans, behaviors):

_____

_____

_____

_____

_____

Others who can help you accomplish this goal:

_____

_____

_____

_____

_____

How you will follow up and know if you are successful:

_____

_____

_____

_____

_____

Conflict Management

INTRODUCTION

We can find conflict everywhere in organizational life, and how we manage conflict reflects on our effectiveness. In this module, you lead the participants as they strengthen and apply the skills learned in modules 1 and 2. As with any lesson, the learning begins with you, the instructor.

INSTRUCTOR PREPARATION

Take time to reflect upon and study the skills and theories regarding conflict management. Chapter 6 in this book lists many resources for teaching conflict management.[1] Your own commitment to continuing development in this area will help your students.

 **Materials**

Assemble these materials before the session.

- ❑ Overhead transparencies or slide show for module 3 with appropriate equipment
- ❑ Two flip-chart pads on easels with markers
- ❑ Flip-chart pages prepared with content and titles
- ❑ Participant workbooks
- ❑ GourmetPet.com and Beloved handouts for workbook activity 3.1
- ❑ Trainer's workshop guide

❏ Participant awards for the conflict game of peril (for example, wrapped candy for each participant and for each member of the winning team a lottery ticket worth up to $20,000; see exercise 3-5 for details)

✓ Checklist

Check the facility carefully before the participants arrive.

❏ Does the equipment work?

❏ Are tables and chairs arranged appropriately?

❏ Are windows, doors, and lighting comfortable?

❏ If the break includes refreshments, are they set up?

❏ Do you know the location of rest rooms and telephones?

❏ Do you know the numbers and contacts for emergency assistance?

❏ Are the flip charts set up with markers?

❏ Are name tents available with markers?

 Facilitator: You can show overhead 3.1 as participants arrive. Full-size overheads are found in appendix A.

> *Conflict Management*
>
> Powerful skills for productive conflict management and resolution
>
> 3.1

Scope and Sequence

In this module the participants extend and apply the skills for listening and assertiveness learned in the first two sessions. The module begins with the distinction between productive and destructive conflict management. Next, the participants identify their conflict style and learn skills for integrative conflict management. Then the trainees apply the principles of conflict management by preparing for a negotiation.

The participants then practice their communication skills for conflict resolution in a series of exercises. In the conflict game of peril group members compete and demonstrate the knowledge they have learned throughout the session. The module's conclusion features an ongoing plan for developing competence in conflict management.

LECTURE NOTES: CONFLICT MANAGEMENT

Total time: 4 hours
Midpoint break: 15 minutes

Introduction

Time for segment: 20 minutes

Begin by telling a story about conflict. As in the following example, your story ought to portray essential characteristics of conflict.

> Recently, a colleague approached me and told me his story, which is rife with conflict. An intelligent, likable, and earnest young man, he is the consummate impressive professional, always dressed in a suit and tie.
>
> He got involved in politics and was upwardly mobile in a large municipal organization. However, as the story turns out, the local government changed leadership after an election. Through a poor series of moves in the organization my colleague was almost destroyed. This story has a sad ending—ultimately he was forced to leave the organization—and my young friend is no longer so innocent. This was a very destructive conflict that harmed both my friend and the organization through a long court battle.

Whatever story you tell, relate the story to the pervasiveness of conflict. Wherever you go you will encounter conflict, and the more involved you become in organizations, the more conflicts you are likely to experience.

Exercise 3.1. Conflict Metaphors

Ask participants to complete the sentence "Conflict is. . . ."

 Facilitator: Prepare a flip-chart page with "Conflict is . . ." across the top.

Ask them to write their answers on the extra note pages provided in their workbooks. Tell them that all answers are good, and instruct them to brainstorm as many metaphors, similes, or types of responses as possible. Encourage everyone to write at least one response.

Ask for their responses and record them on the flip chart. Acknowledge and summarize their perspectives. Then relate their perspectives to the importance of managing conflict effectively. How important is it to be competent at conflict management?

Facilitator: Show overheads 3.2 and 3.3.

Conflict Archetypes

- Warrior
  - Is impeccable, competent.
  - Confronts and empathizes.
- Saint
  - Offers forgiveness, change of perspective.
  - Alters self and relationships.

3.2

Conflict Archetypes (Cont.)

- Teacher
  - Reframes.
  - Helps others develop, including opponents.
- Student
  - Seeks continuous self-development.

3.3

Provide the metaphors for conflict management skills. Explain how conflict challenges us to develop according to the archetypes outlined in the overheads. The impeccable *warrior* fully develops his or her capacity to confront and to empathize with others. The person who masters conflict management must also have the power to forgive others like a *saint*. Someone who excels at conflict management is also a *teacher,* who, in turn, helps foster these skills in others. The final archetype is the *student* who strives to learn constantly from every conflict situation.

Next, introduce the session's agenda and objectives.

 Facilitator: Display and read overheads 3.4, 3.5, and 3.6.

In this session, we will cover five skills, or competencies, for managing conflict. These are

---

Module Agenda

- Total time: Four hours
- Conflict styles and strategies
- Integrative conflict management
- Negotiation planning
- Communication skills and cases

3.4

Module Agenda (Cont.)

- Break: Fifteen Minutes
- Communication skills and cases (continued)
- Third-party intervention
- Development in conflict management

3.5

Module Objectives

Conflict style and strategy — Negotiation preparation — Conflict management — Communication skills — Third-party intervention

3.6

conflict styles and strategies, integrative conflict management, negotiation preparation, communication skills for conflict management, and third-party intervention.

Inform the participants that toward the end of the module they will play a game, the conflict game of peril. In this game they will be tested, in teams, to see how much they have learned throughout the session. Tell them rewards will be enormous—up to $20,000 (or whatever amount the lottery is paying that week)—and to pay attention!

 Training Tip: The Conflict Game of Peril

From time to time and humorously, if possible, remind the participants of the upcoming conflict game of peril. Anticipating this game will make learning more fun and provide an incentive to learn the material. You can point out this game will also demonstrate competition between teams and collaboration within teams. In addition, the game provides you with a formative evaluation for the module for you will get to see how well the participants have learned the material.

Conflict Styles and Strategies

Time for segment: 25 minutes

Conflict is ubiquitous in everyday life. Just read the headlines in any paper or listen to the television news. Take a good look at any organization. Examine your own life.

How many of you have a good clash going on in your own life right now? Knowing how to deal with conflict effectively is crucial to success in almost any sphere of life. Conflict can be either destructive or constructive. It can sometimes tear an organization or a relationship apart, leading to rigidity and ineffectiveness. If you manage it well, however, conflict is constructive, leading to learning, change, and improved effectiveness. Learning how to manage conflict well is an asset for all of us.

 Facilitator: Display and read overheads 3.7 and 3.8.

Conflict Defined	*Conflict Defined (Cont.)*

• Conflict occurs when interdependent people pursue goals or values and perceive interference from one another.	• Key concepts:
	  • Interdependence
	  • Goals or values
	  • Perception
	  • Interference

3.7	3.8

Let's define conflict: *Conflict* occurs when interdependent people pursue goals or values and perceive interference from one another. First, we see conflict happens primarily among people who depend on one another or work closely together. For example, in the United States the most common violence is domestic violence, which occurs within the home.

Conflict emerges among people who want to pursue *goals or values.* Here *perception* is important, particularly the perception of *interference.* While these people might not encounter actual interference, their perception of interference is often enough to start a conflict.

In this session, we will learn several skills for managing conflict. The first involves recognizing conflict styles.

Conflict styles

 Facilitator: Explain the conflict management style grid as you show overhead 3.9.

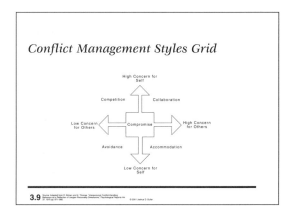

The conflict management styles grid represents a way to understand and prepare for conflict. The grid has two axes—concern for the self and concern for others, which increase from low to high along each axis.

Let's look at each style by using them in an example. Say a new position opens in a corporation, and two employees who know each other decide to apply for it. Each one wants the job, and when they find out the other wants it, too, each perceives interference from the other.

They would be *avoiding* their conflict if they did not discuss their perceived interference. Sometimes avoiding conflict is good, particularly if the relationship and the issue are not important, but at other times, it is destructive to avoid conflict. This lapse in communication shows a lack of concern for oneself and others. The relationship is diminished by this lack of communication. Not communicating during a conflict can breed negativity. Generally, if two people are interdependent and they avoid conflict, then their conflict becomes destructive.

One person could decide to *accommodate* the other by withdrawing from the race and letting the other person have the job. Accommodation is a good move if the person did not really want the job and wanted to invest in the relationship with his coworker. If he really wants the job and accommodates the other person, however, then he is undermining himself. Such a lack of assertiveness can lead to resentment, which weakens the relationship.

A third option is *competition,* which involves a high concern for oneself and a low concern for the other. As in sports and in many areas of business, the objective is to win one for the team while the other team loses. Such competition can backfire with coworkers. Remember that each victory contains the seeds of defeat. What if one contender for the new position wins and the other perceives him as deceptive or manipulative? The loser might sabotage the winner later.

Another option is *compromise,* in which each party's gain is cut in half so that each person is treated equally and gets an equal share. For the job seekers, one solution might be a job sharing so that both people do the same work. Another compromise involves tossing a coin to see who gets the position. Neither a coin toss nor job sharing is the best solution, because neither identifies the best candidate for the job. The standards for such decision making are nominal—and not based on performance.

I believe the best option in this circumstance is *collaboration.* In collaboration, as in teamwork, both parties focus on the goals of the organization. Collaboration means having a high concern for self, others, and the organization. The most advantageous results the organization are that the best candidate gets the job and that the hiring committee applies objective criteria to select the most qualified candidate. A collaborative climate would feature supportive and open communication—both confrontation and empathy. Collaboration in this circumstance can maintain understanding between the two applicants no matter who was selected. Collaboration would also ensure the selection of the best candidate, which serves the organization's best interests.

 Faciltator: Keep overhead 3.9 on display.

Exercise 3.2. Conflict Management Styles

Next, help the participants identify the conflict styles they tend to use.

Although we each might use different styles in different situations, many of us prefer one style over others. We will do an exercise in which you identify your preferred style.

1. Think about a current or past conflict. What conflict comes to mind?

2. Write down the name of the other person involved in the conflict.

3. Now reflect on your behavior in this conflict, and write down the name of the conflict style that best describes your behavior.

Give them enough time to identify their conflict style. Next, instruct the participants to use the conflict management styles overhead as a top view of the room and to move to the part of the room that represents their conflict management style. Collaborators will meet at the front right, competitors at the front left, the compromising group in the middle, the accommodation group at the back right, and the avoidance group at the back left. Point and help the participants find their groups.

▶ Training Tip: A Lighthearted Moment

Training sessions can seem long, and it is good to get the participants up and moving about from time to time. It keeps them interested, alert, and ready to learn. For these reasons it is a good idea to have people stand as they group together.

> Let's hear from each group. In an informal way, I would like each group to identify someone who will say a few words to the class about the group's conflict style. Say anything you would like to explain the style—its nature, costs, or benefits.

Give the groups about a minute to interact, and then call for everyone's attention. Ask to hear from each group. More than one person may speak. Usually, their comments will reveal something about their style; for example, competitors will be concerned about winning. Use each group's examples to illustrate the style's characteristics. Responses from different groups might overlap, and some people may feel they use a variety of styles in different situations. Acknowledge the experience of participants. Then ask everyone to sit down.

Debrief the exercise. Ask the participants for their comments and evaluations of the conflict management style grid. Steer the conversation toward the following points:

1. Many of us alternate styles depending on the situation.
2. We have to be selective, for any of the five styles might be the most effective given our goals in a particular situation.
3. The model enables us to analyze a conflict and determine the styles we want to use to accomplish our goals.
4. We are most effective when we are flexible and able to use any of the five styles to meet our purpose.
5. The most difficult style might be collaboration, but it is the most promising. We discuss collaboration further in the next section.

Integrative Conflict Management

Time for this segment: 15 minutes

Participants often have a difficult time distinguishing between compromise and collaboration. Deliberating this question is a good place to launch your discussion of collaboration, or integrative conflict management.

Facilitator: Display and explain overheads 3.10 and 3.11: Distributive versus Integrative Conflict Management.

Disbributive versus Integrative Conflict Management

Distributive	Integrative
Win-lose	Win-win
Competition = Zero-sum game $+1 - 1 = 0$	Collaboration = Nonzero-sum game $+1 + 1 = 2$
Compromise = $+ \frac{1}{2} - \frac{1}{2} + \frac{1}{2} - \frac{1}{2} = 0$	

3.10

Distributive versus Integrative Conflict Management (Cont.)

Distributive	Integrative
Trade-offs, fixed-sum issues, and limited resources	Creative solutions, overlapping interests, and variable-sum issues
Withholding information, deception, seeking information	Open communication, information sharing, shared inquiry

3.11

In a win-lose conflict, parties avoid, accommodate, compete, or compromise. In accommodation, one party often gives in and loses. If the losing party's interests were not served, the downside is. the loser might respond passive-aggressively and undermine the winning party later. Accommodation is a *zero-sum game:* Plus one for the winner and minus one for the loser equals zero.

Competition—with one party losing and one party winning—is similar. The sum is zero. Interestingly, compromise is the same. Because each party wins one-half and loses one-half, the total is zero. Collaboration, which requires assertiveness by both parties, has the greatest potential return. If both parties can win, then it becomes a nonzero-sum game. One win plus one win amounts to two satisfied parties.

Distributive conflict management, with its winners and losers, has no room for creativity. Issues are fixed, with one traded off for another, and resources are treated as limited. Communication in distributive conflict management is closed. Each person wants to win at the other's expense and therefore withholds information, seeks information from the other, and deceives where possible.

In contrast, *integrative conflict management* seeks creative solutions, overlapping interests, and variable-sum issues. Creative solutions bring new and useful ideas. For instance, labor might make a concession in collective bargaining they had not previously imagined. This concession might get them something they want, such as increased wages, by giving something they don't mind giving, such as increased productivity. An example of overlapping interests is two managers who have a turf battle, but realize they both would benefit from hiring an external consultant to research the issue. Similarly, variable-sum issues means that parties consider additional issues as part of the negotiation. Coworkers that disagree about scheduling in the office might consider telecommuting. Parties communicate openly, sharing and seeking information. Rather than avoiding communication or being aggressive, the parties assert themselves and confront one another with empathy in a supportive climate.

Some of you might be skeptical about integrative conflict management. What could go wrong with it? Some people seem incapable of collaboration, but by preparing yourself in this management style, you increase the chances both that others will choose to collaborate with you and that your conflict resolution will be constructive rather than destructive.

Success in conflict management requires a strategy and an array of communication tools. The next segment covers the strategic preparation for conflict management.

Negotiation Preparation

Time for this segment: 30 minutes

Integrative conflict management involves negotiations in which two parties with conflicting interests attempt to resolve or at least manage their differences through constructive conversation. If we stop and think about it, we negotiate our way through life. We negotiate our salaries, the cost of each other's services, and our roles at work and at home.

Whether our negotiations with others are spur-of-the-moment or truly momentous, one principle holds true: Effective negotiators stop and take the time to think and to plan. This preparation is the most important step in managing any conflict.

Facilitator: Show and review overhead 3.12: Negotiation Preparation Worksheet I.

> **Negotiation Preparation Worksheet I**
>
> Your interests:
>
> Their interests:
>
> Creative options:
>
> Your best option other than negotiating:
>
> The least you will live with:
>
> 3.12

Preparation for negotiation consists of:

- Analyzing interests—yours and theirs
- Generating creative solutions
- Determining your best option other than negotiating
- Identifying the least you can live with in the negotiation

Let's work through an example. Imagine you work as a supply chain buyer in a computer manufacturing organization. You manage the relationship with ProFormatica, the company that makes the plastic casings for your computers. Recently both companies have complained about this relationship. You took some time to analyze this situation, and here is what you found.

*Facilitator: Show overhead 3.13:
Negotiation Preparation Worksheet II and
explain both parties' interests.*

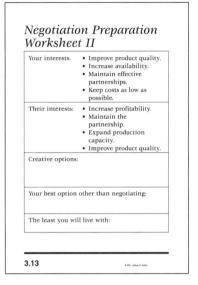

To prepare for negotiation and conflict, it is crucial to review your interests. Knowing your interests is the key to staying focused and to being successful. Maintaining your interests is a good measure of your performance as a negotiator.

Next, determine the other party's interests. Sometimes you need to use your imagination; however, don't let it run amok. In conflict situations, we often imagine the worst about the other party, which does not help the tone of the conversation. Use your imagination to understand the other party's interests, but be as tangible and down-to-earth as possible.

Here is what Abraham Lincoln had to say about contention:

When I am getting ready to reason with a man,
I spend one-third of my time thinking about myself and what I am going to say and two-thirds about him and what he is going to say.

 *Facilitator: Display and read overhead
3.14. Explain its creative options.*

Creative options expand the possibilities. Look for what else can you do to solve your problem. Your first idea is to help ProFormatica achieve their highest-ranked interest, profitability. From that idea flows synergy among all of these features—increased profitability comes with increased automation, which also improves availability and quality.

Here are some general approaches to creative solutions:

1. Create a climate for new possibilities with new ideas, people, attitudes, situations, and conversations.

2. Brainstorm as many ideas as you can.

3. Generate a creative climate by asking the question, What if?

4. Expand your possibilities by identifying additional sources of such resources as money, people, and time.

5. Look for superordinate values, which bring your interests together on a higher level.

The next step is to determine your best option other than negotiating. This initiative represents your alternative to working with this partner. For example, you could find a new partner, or you could manufacture the parts in-house. An alternative gives you power and objectivity in negotiations.

Next, determine your best outcomes from this negotiation. The only limits here are basic to integrative negotiation: You have to satisfy your partner's minimum interests. For example, your partner's nonnegotiable bottom line is that ProFormatica needs to be profitable to remain in business. Also, you want to maintain the relationship.

The last step is deciding what is the least you will live with. It needs to be at least a little better than what you determined was your best option other than negotiating.

Evaluate this preparation. What is missing? What could go wrong? What could happen if you did not prepare?

Steer the participants toward the realization that preparation aids collaboration. Emphasize that the synergy in this example could be wasted if the partners are accommodating or competitive rather than collaborative.

Now we will prepare for negotiation by working a case study with partners. I would like you to turn to workbook activity 3.1. You will work in pairs.

Count off the participants in pairs. You need an even number of pairs. If necessary, make a group of three people.

This negotiation consists of an acquisition of GourmetPet.com, an e-business company, by the large pet food company Beloved Incorporated. Identify each pair as representing either GourmetPet.com or Beloved Incorporated. A copy of the worksheet appears in the workbook materials. Hand out your photocopies of the case studies, taking care to let each pair see only their own handout.

 Facilitator: Hand out the case studies.

Give the participants fifteen minutes to read the handout and prepare for their negotiations. Check in with the groups to see if they are making progress.

After the groups have completed their preparation worksheet in their workbooks, tell them to save these materials for later. They will use them in a negotiation, but first they need to consider the communication tools for integrative conflict management.

NEGOTIATION PREPARATION

You will prepare for a negotiation. In this negotiation you will represent either GourmetPet.com or Beloved Incorporated. Read the case, and in the worksheet below plan your negotiation with your partner.

Your interests:
Their interests:
Creative options:
Your best option other than negotiating:
The least you will live with:

Case Study

Team 1. Owners of GourmetPet.com

You and your partner founded an e-business, GourmetPet.com, that retails gourmet food for pets. A large pet food company called Beloved Incorporated wants to buy your company.

You are interested in selling the company because you want the cash. However, you feel attached to the employees in the company and to the unique company culture. You want the forty-five employees to retain their jobs. Also, you both are willing to stay on in a general management position for three years, with average annual salaries of $350,000, to help with the transition. Given revenues and profit growth, you believe the company is worth $5 million. Company revenues were $4 million last year, and profits were 8 percent.

In early negotiations you and your partner have determined that Beloved wants to pay $3 million as up-front money for the purchase, although there are other avenues to provide payment over time. You also understand that Beloved would like you both to stay in management positions; however, they want an escape clause to terminate your positions if deemed necessary.

Case Study

Team 2. Chief Negotiators for Beloved Incorporated

You and your partners are Beloved Incorporated's chief negotiators in the company's bid to acquire GourmetPet.com. Your executive team sees the acquisition as a key strategy in taking market share in the new economy.

Due to a shortage of capital, you do not want to invest more than $3 million up front to acquire GourmetPet.com. You are, however, open to other means of payment over time.

You are aware that the owners of GourmetPet.com have created a unique corporate culture, and you are willing to let them remain in management positions with a contract for the next three years. You do want a cancellation clause, in the event that the current owners do not work out with Beloved Incorporated. You are willing to negotiate the conditions of this clause.

You want to acquire the company as soon as possible. Also, you want to keep the management salaries in line with Beloved's norms, which for such proposed positions would be less than $300,000 per year.

Communication Skills for Conflict Management

Time for segment: 30 minutes

Communication skills might be likened to tools in a toolbox. If you only know how to use a hammer, then everything in life looks like a nail. If you learn how to use the other tools in the box, then you have greater options and can search for the right tool for the job. The more skills and knowledge you have, the greater your chances for effectiveness in complex organizations.

 Facilitator: Display and read overhead 3.15.

Preview the communication skills for conflict management. These communication skills build on the skills from the first two sessions—listening and assertiveness.

What to do before the conversation

 Facilitator: Display and read in your own words overhead 3.16. Emphasize the first point—cool off.

In integrative conflict management, you gain no advantage in reacting emotionally. A contentious adversary will take your loss of cool as a sign of weakness and exploit it. What other preparations would you make before starting the conversation?

Communication Skills

- What to do before the conversation
- Conversational skills and insights:
  - Making "I statements"
  - Confirming the other person's point of view
  - Responding to attacks
  - Dealing with fallacies
- Third-party intervention

3.15

What to Do before the Conversation

- Cool off.
- Find a convenient time.
- Prepare.
- Set the tone for a constructive purpose.
- Review supportive and defensive climates and communication skills.

3.16

Conversational skills and insights

In integrative conflict management, you resolve and manage conflicts in ways that satisfy both parties' interests. To accomplish this negotiation, you must master a set of tools. While the other person might fail to integrate his or her interests with yours, you can use your tools to integrate your interests.

Such work requires a mastery of communication skills, which might require extensive development, but with experience the competent communicator knows what negotiation tools work and which do not. Communication in integrative conflict management consists of four tools:

1. Using I statements
2. Confirming their point of view
3. Responding to attacks
4. Responding to fallacies

Confrontation starts when people express different experiences and interests. The philosopher Martin Buber referred to this aspect of dialogue as "the essential courage" and "one person up against the other."[2] Confrontation is necessary in conflict management. If you cannot express your interests, you cannot effectively manage or resolve conflict.

I statements are a way to express your interests directly without evoking unnecessary defensiveness in your partner. By using I statements we take ownership of our feelings and our position, which makes it much easier for the other person to listen to us. I statements increase the chance that your partner will respond positively to your interests.

 Facilitator: Display and explain overheads 3.17 and 3.18.

In using I statements, first we must establish ownership of our interests. Whenever you say "you are," you make your listener defensive. By saying "I feel" or "I don't like," you reduce the listener's defensiveness. Defensiveness easily leads to anger. And if you want the other party to listen, really listen, to your side, you don't make that person mad. Ideally, we should be able to say the whole I statement without using the word *you.*

I Statements

Example: I feel frustrated with the lack of progress on this project. I get worried when I see that four of your assignments are overdue. I am interested in determining commitments to action assignments today because I want us to complete this project on time and according to plan.

3.17   © 2001 Joshua D. Guilar

I Statements (Cont.)

Example language for the four steps
"I feel . . . when I . . . I would like you to . . . because . . ."
"I think . . . when you . . . I need . . . the goal . . ."
"I believe . . . when the . . . I want . . . our interests . . ."
"I don't like . . . to be the . . . I wish . . . so I can . . ."

3.19   © 2001 Joshua D. Guilar

Facilitator: Display overhead 3.19.

> **I Statements (Cont.)**
>
> • Four-step format
>   • Ownership—"I feel frustrated with the lack of progress on this project."
>   • Problem—"I get worried when I see that four of your assignments are overdue."
>   • Intermediate goal—"I am interested in determining commitments to action assignments today."
>   • End goal—"because I want us to complete this project on time and according to plan."
>
> ───────────────────────────
> 3.18   © 2001 Joshua D. Guilar

Sometimes, however, we cannot avoid using the word *you* when describing our problem, and that is okay.

In the second step, describe the behavior you believe causes the problem. Use descriptive rather than judgmental language. Be as concrete and nonjudgmental as possible. The example on the overhead is "Four of your assignments are overdue."

The next step describes what you would like to happen. Often it is the concrete behavior you would like from the other person. For example, say, "I would like you to arrive at the meetings at six o'clock." Avoid being vague, because that only sets up the other person to fail. Note the difference between asking someone to [quote] "improve their communication" [unquote] and asking someone to [quote] "inform you of changes to the schedule immediately as changes occur." [unquote]

The final step is to refer to the higher-order interests behind this confrontation. This goal is something you would like to correct or, better yet, something that both you and your partner would like to correct.

 Facilitator: Read the following case to the participants.

Ask the participants to write an I statement for the case on Workbook Activity 3.2. Give them four minutes. When they finish, ask the participants to share their work in pairs. Everyone tells their partners their I statements. Then the partners critique each others' statement. Did they feel defensive? Did the statement conform to the four-step model?

Next, ask the participants to share what they find to be a workable I statement with the whole group. The volunteers—or people you call on—role-play their scenes for the group. Acknowledge and critique the statements until the participants satisfy the assignment. Then transition to the next tool, which is confirming the other person's point of view.

Confrontation and empathy are not mutually exclusive. On the contrary, they are synergistic, with empathy leading to more effective confrontation. *Empathy* is imagining what a situation looks like from the other person's point of view. William Ury describes empathy as "stepping to the other side."[3]

Listening for understanding is evidence of empathy and what psychologist Carl Rogers called "unconditional positive regard."[4] Showing empathy does not mean we agree with a person or that we have surrendered our interests. It means that, at least for a while, we simply suspend our interests in order to support and understand the other person's perspective and interests.

I STATEMENTS

In this activity you will design and communicate an I statement based on the following scenario.

You have a conflict with your manager, Jack. You have already negotiated with Jack for travel funds to visit a crucial customer in California. Earlier, Jack had agreed to your trip, and you told your customer to expect you. Now Jack has turned down your travel request and did not mention your earlier agreement. You have decided to confront Jack on this issue.

Write your I statement in the space below. Remember the formula:

1. Ownership—"I feel frustrated with the progress on this project."
2. Problem—"I get worried when I see that four of our assignments are overdue."
3. Intermediate goal—"I am interested in determining commitments to action assignments today."
4. End goal—"because we need to complete this project on time and according to plan."

I Statement:

_____

_____

_____

_____

_____

_____

_____

_____

_____

Paradoxically, empathy, or imagining the other person's point of view, requires great confidence. Supreme Court Justice Oliver Wendell Holmes once said, "The sign of a civilized man is his willingness to give up his most cherished beliefs." It takes great confidence to be open to learning in confrontation. Being able to shift from our own perspective on the conflict to see the other side encourages the other person to shift their perspective, also. This mutual openness is a characteristic of true dialogue. Altering our respective views of the relationship, for a while, enables our relationship to change from both sides. This force is perhaps the strongest for resolving conflict.

 Facilitator: Display overhead 3.20.

What we say to the other party helps our conscious choice to suspend our interests and to remain open to change. Here are some steps for confirming the other person's point of view:

> *Confirming the Other Person's Point of View*
>
> • Slow down the process.
> • Shift to the other person's point of view.
> • Imagine what the other person thinks and feels.
> • Ask a constructive question.
> • Confirm the person's experience.
> • Offer to help as appropriate.
> • Continue to negotiate.
>
> 3.20   © 2001 Joshua D. Guilar

1. Slow down the process. Take time out. Take a breath, particularly when you encounter a negative tone.

2. Shift your thinking and feeling away from yourself and toward the other person's experience. This process takes an act of will.

3. Ask a constructive question if you lack information (but don't ask in the spirit of inquisition).

4. Imagine what the other person thinks and feels. Take another deep breath.

5. Confirm the person's feelings, experience, and perspective. Act confidently as you do this. Remember you are not agreeing with the other person's reasons, and you are not surrendering your interests or your principles.

6. Offer to help as appropriate.

7. Continue to negotiate.

 Facilitator: Instruct participants to complete workbook activity 3.3.

When they are done, ask the participants to share their scripts. Acknowledge participants' work, which can be very diverse in approach. Also use this opportunity to summarize skills for integrative conflict management.

CONFIRMING THE OTHER PERSON'S POINT OF VIEW

In workbook activity 3.2, you used an I statement to confront your manager, Jack. Unfortunately, in this next scenario, Jack responds defensively. After you pose your I statement, Jack retorts, "No, you cannot go to California, and that is that."

Remember the steps for confirming his point of view:

1. Take time to slow down the process. Take a breath.
2. Shift your thinking and feeling away from yourself and toward Jack's experience. Use your will power.
3. Imagine what he feels and thinks.
4. Ask a constructive question if you need information.
5. Confirm Jack's feelings, experience, and perspective. Acknowledge them. Act confidently as you do this for you are not surrendering your interests or your principles.
6. Offer to help Jack as appropriate.
7. Continue to negotiate.

Part 1. Information

In the space below, write what you would say for step 4 above.

Ask for more information:

_____

_____

_____

_____

_____

_____

_____

Part 2. Perspective and Help

Jack responds, "This is just a tough time for me right now. I do not have time to analyze your request. I'm sorry to say we might be over the budget this month. I do not know if we can afford this expense just now."

In the space below, write what you would say for steps 5 and 6. Remember you are not surrendering your interests or your principles.

Acknowledge perspective and offer help:

_____

_____

_____

_____

_____

_____

_____

_____

_____

Now that you have confirmed and understood Jack's point of view, you are ready to continue the negotiation. Write how you would continue this negotiation in the space below.

Continue to negotiate:

_____

_____

_____

_____

_____

_____

_____

_____

Midpoint Break

Time for break: **15 minutes**

Clearly state your expectations about starting on time after the break. After the break you will cover communication skills for conflict management.

Communication Skills for Conflict Management (Continued)

Time for segment: 30 minutes

Next, we will study how to respond to an attack. Say you are negotiating a contract, and the other side calls you selfish and deceitful. Their tone is emotional. What do you do?

When attacked, most of us react emotionally. An emotional reaction is natural, but it is rarely productive.

Facilitator: Display and read the guidelines on overhead 3.21. Give examples and model the behaviors.

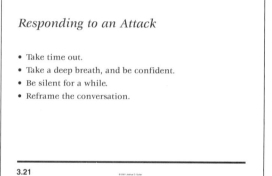

Responding to an Attack

- Take time out.
- Take a deep breath, and be confident.
- Be silent for a while.
- Reframe the conversation.

3.21

Here are guidelines for dealing with an attack:

1. Take time out to make sure that you act rather than react.

2. Try being silent for a while, and let the other person speak.

3. Reframe the conversation toward the interests you both have at stake.

If you are reacting emotionally, take the time to collect yourself. Listen to how you feel and react. Take a deep breath. Remind yourself to be confident. In some circumstances, you can take a break. In any case, a good idea is to be silent for a while. Your silence puts the onus on the other person to keep talking. The person might even get embarrassed. Taking a break gives you a chance to analyze the conversation clearly. As William Ury says, "Don't get mad, don't get even—get what you want."[5]

Identify the person's communication for what it is—an attack. Martial artists use the other person's attack to reposition both parties. Try this technique, and see that the other person is off balance, or "out of integrity." An attack is not constructive. Do not use this opportunity to counterattack; rather, redirect the conversation toward constructive issues. Reframe it by returning to your interests and the interests of the other party by saying something like, "We both have interests at stake here, and I want to return to what we want to accomplish in this conversation."

Facilitator: Instruct the group to turn to workbook activity 3.4.

RESPONDING TO AN ATTACK

In this activity, you will respond to a verbal attack. Imagine this scenario.

You are an advertising consultant in a small advertising agency. Your manager has asked you and a fellow consultant, Chris, to direct a project. Unfortunately, you do not get along with Chris. You feel Chris blocks your ideas, tells you what to do, and is trying to control the project and make you his go-for—someone who follows his instructions.

You decide to approach Chris, and he agrees to discuss your work relationship. You start by saying you want to collaborate and have an equal role with Chris. To that end, you need to establish standards for your work together.

Chris responds, "You have got to be kidding. I have worked here twice as long as you have, and I certainly do not intend to take orders from you."

Dialogue 1. Responding to an Attack

Remember the guidelines for dealing with an attack:

1. Take time out to make sure you act rather than react.
2. Try being silent for a while.
3. Reframe the conversation toward the interests that you both have at stake—in this case, the successful completion of the project.

In the space below, describe how you would respond to Chris. Follow the guidelines for responding to an attack.

Your response:

_____

_____

_____

_____

_____

_____

_____

_____

_____

_____

_____

_____

_____

_____

_____

_____

_____

_____

_____

_____

_____

_____

This conversation continues in the next workbook activity on dealing with fallacies.

In this activity, the participants work in pairs and create a role-play. Here are the instructions:

1. Form the participants into pairs.

2. Give them six minutes to read the case and to write their dialogue in the space provided.

3. Ask for volunteers to role-play their dialogue for the whole group. Have one person play the role of Chris, who listens at first and then agrees to change, and have the other person read the script he or she wrote for the workbook activity.

4. Acknowledge and critique their work. In the role-plays it should become apparent that fine-tuning the language makes a big difference in reducing defensiveness.

5. Work with examples until a volunteer follows the guidelines and achieves the goals of the role-play.

Debrief the exercise. Then direct the participants to the next topic.

People often communicate with smoke screens, deceptions, tricks, and fallacies. Seeing these devices for what they are enables you to manage conflict well in tough situations.

Reasoning is a conclusion linked logically to evidence. A *fallacy* is an error in reasoning. For your conclusion to be sound, you must support it with evidence, and the link between the two must be logical. In managing conflict and in solving any problem, it is important that you base your communication on valid data. Also, you have to be able to recognize fallacies, question them, and steer the conversation with the objective criteria of reason and valid data.

 Facilitator: Display and explain overhead 3.22.

Dealing with Fallacies

- Recognize the fallacy for what it is.
- Question its logic and data.
- Reframe based on valid logic and data.

3.22

Say you present an idea for a new product in a meeting. A coworker sniffs, "That'll never work. We tried that two years ago, and it failed." What kind of fallacy are you encountering here?

There are many kinds of fallacies. Here are some examples:

1. *Ad hominem.* In Latin this means "against the man." To attack the person rather than address the issue is an error in reasoning. Authors Fisher, Ury, and Patton have argued for the depersonalization of conflict management, or to "separate the people from the problem."[6]

2. *Inferential thinking.* An *inference* is a jump from the known to the unknown. For example, person A observes that person B has been late for work the last two days. However, any assumption that person A makes about person B being lazy, for instance, is just an inference. Perhaps person B has been visiting his or her spouse in the hospital. Person A should inquire rather than assume.

3. *Red herring.* This metaphor is from Britain, where farmers used to rub a smoked fish around their fields to keep animals away from their crops. Identifying the real issues and relevant data are crucial in conflict management.

4. *Either-or.* Often someone in a conflict will claim there are only two options, whereas there might be many more.

Many more types of fallacies abound. In conflict, learn to think clearly and critically. Look for fallacies and intervene as appropriate. Ask questions. What is being omitted? What is being fabricated? Does the conclusion necessarily follow from the claims? What other conclusions could be reached?

As James Carse said, "To be prepared against surprise is to be trained. To be prepared for surprise is to be educated." Once you are have learned the skills, you can recognize the fallacious argument and prevent it from hindering your success.

 Facilitator: Ask participants to read workbook activity 3.5.

Ask the participants to fill in their responses to the fallacy. Give them six minutes, and check their progress. When they are finished, debrief the exercise. Ask the participants for examples until you find one that satisfies the guidelines.

Negotiation Process
Time for segment: 25 minutes

Exercise 3.3. Negotiation between GourmetPet.com and Beloved Incorporated

Up to this point, the participants have studied conflict styles and analysis, preparation for negotiation, and communication skills for conflict management. Next, they apply all of these skills in a negotiation.

Review the negotiation preparation the participants did in workbook activity 3.1. Instruct the participants to reassemble into the same teams and to follow the steps on overhead 3.23.

DEALING WITH FALLACIES

Chris responds to your intervention and appears to listen. He agrees to accommodate your interests, to collaborate with you, and to treat you as an equal.

Now you tackle the project itself to see how this new collaboration works. You meet with Chris again to make a decision on the storyboards for the advertising project. Both of you have been working on storyboards, and each of you brings an idea to the meeting. You take turns presenting your ideas.

After both presentations Chris says, "Your idea will never work. People just aren't attracted to this kind of thing." You disagree and believe your market research justifies your ideas.

In the space below, describe how you would respond to Chris. Remember the guidelines for dealing with fallacies:

1. Recognize the fallacy for what it is.
2. Question the logic and data.
3. Reframe the conversation based on valid logic and data.

Your response:

Facilitator: Display overhead 3.23.

After the GourmetPet.com and Beloved pairs have assembled in their negotiation groups, monitor the groups closely. They have five minutes to prepare in pairs and fifteen minutes to negotiate. After negotiations, ask them for feedback about the process. Relate their comments back to the skills learned throughout the session. Then move to the next segment.

> *Negotiation Process*
>
> - Form back into negotiation teams.
> - Review preparation: five minutes.
> - Meet with alliance partners in the other organization.
> - Negotiate an agreement, or not: fifteen minutes.
> - Record your agreement.
> - Debrief and evaluate your negotiation process.
>
> 3.23

Exercise 3.4. Third-Party Intervention

Includes Workbook Activity 3.6. Third-Party Intervention

In a *third-party intervention,* the disputants engage a third party to help them resolve their conflict. The role of the third party must be clear. As a facilitator, the third party simply helps the two sides with their communication, allowing the disputants to make their own decisions. In this exercise about third-party intervention, the facilitator's role is to apply the knowledge and skills learned throughout this session.

Managers skilled in third-party intervention help team members resolve conflicts. Also, they can further serve their teams by teaching them conflict management and resolution skills.

 Training Tip: Managing Time

Check the time. You need at least fifty minutes to conduct the upcoming conflict game of peril and to conclude the session. Expand the segment on third-party intervention based on the time available. If time is short, just read the two overheads on third-party intervention and summarize the information. If more time is available, then do the workbook activity in detail.

 Facilitator: Display and read overheads 3.24 and 3.25.

> *Third-Party Intervention*
>
> | Topic | Relevance |
> |---|---|
> | • Conflict styles | • Assertiveness
• Integrative conflict management
• Collaboration |
> | • Preparation | • Know interests of both parties.
• Prepare creative solutions. |
>
> 3.24

> *Third-Party Intervention (Cont.)*
>
> | Topic | Relevance |
> |---|---|
> | • Responding to attacks | • Cool off and respond; do not react. |
> | • Responding to fallacies | • Set standards for valid information and decisions. |
> | • Reducing defensiveness | • Use open communication and shared inquiry. |
>
> 3.25

THIRD-PARTY INTERVENTION

Role 1. Manager, or Third Party

You are the manager of a marketing department in a large division of a Fortune 50 company. Two of your people—David, who has worked for the department for fifteen years, and Cynthia, who has worked for the company for two years—are having a conflict. They have agreed to meet with you and discuss their work relationship. Your plan for the meeting follows:

1. Discuss the guidelines for integrative conflict management and secure each party's agreement.

2. Use these guidelines to facilitate their conversation.

3. State the objective: To improve understanding and the work relationship between David and Cynthia.

4. Have each party express their interests, or what they would like to ask of the other person (begin with Cynthia).

5. Give each person a chance to speak until understood by the other person.

6. Reach an agreement on how to manage or resolve the conflict.

7. Agree on a follow-up plan.

Role 2. David

You have agreed to play the role of David in an improvisational role-play. Read the following carefully. Try to make the points in the list below during the role-play conversation. In your role, respond positively to your manager's intervention and when your manager asks you to change.

General information. You have worked for the organization for fifteen years. You know the organization's culture and its processes, and you are deeply committed to the company's mission. You have a bachelor's degree in management.

Your feelings about Cynthia follow:

1. You believe she is very selfish.
2. You have heard that she treats others of lower status with disrespect. (You heard this secondhand from an administrative assistant).
3. She is pushing a project through the department that has not been discussed with the whole team. You want her to talk about the project with the team.
4. You do not trust her.

Role 3. Cynthia

You have agreed to play the role of Cynthia in an improvisational role-play. Read the following carefully. Try to make the points in the list below during the role-play conversation. In your role, respond positively to your manager's intervention and when your manager asks you to change.

General information. You are new in the department. You have finished a master's degree in marketing, and you are eager to make your mark. The manager has asked you to design a marketing strategy for a new product. You are working hard to achieve excellence; however, you feel that some people in the department, particularly David, do not like you.

1. You would like David not to interrupt you when you speak at meetings.
2. You would like to have a supportive and collaborative work environment without the bad feelings you sense at present.

Explain third-party intervention—integrative conflict management based on collaboration and dialogue—and then review the overheads. These topics summarize the guidelines for communication and conflict resolution. Third parties use these same guidelines to intervene and teach during a conflict resolution session.

 Facilitator: Display overhead 3.26.

Agreements

Collaborative climate
  Listening for understanding
  Shared information
  Confirming their point of view
Focus on interest and creative solutions
Valid information and decisions
  Objectively verifiable data
  Reason—conclusions based on evidence and logic
  Inferences and opinions when presented as such

3.26   © 2001 Joshua D. Guilar

Overhead 3.26 shows the agreements required for the conflict resolution session. Review these agreements with the group. In the following role-plays, the third party explains the rules to two disputants and asks them to agree to these guidelines. The agreements can be amended, but both disputants must accept the agreements before moving ahead.

Next, form the participants into groups of three people each. Ask each member of the group to assume a role—the manager, or interventionist; David; and Cynthia. Then instruct them to turn to workbook activity 3.6, which has a case study guide for each actor, and to read only their own role-play page. Each group will then perform the role-play.

Alternate option. Act out this role-play in front of the group. Ask for volunteers or select three people for the roles. Let them improvise their roles, with coaching from you. Display overhead 3.26 with the guidelines for their reference. Inform the role players that you will call time-out occasionally, so the rest of the group can make comments. Also, the time-outs give you a chance to coach the role players on their improvisation.

Debrief after the role-play. How did the manager teach the disputants to follow the agreements? How much progress was made on the dispute? Why? When complete, transition to the game that follows.

Exercise 3.5. The Conflict Game of Peril

For the participants, the conflict game of peril provides an opportunity to review the session's important points. For you, the trainer, observe carefully how much of the material participants know and use their performances as your formative evaluation. After the session, make notes about what they learned and what they did not.

Facilitator:Display overheads 3.27 and 3.28. Explain carefully the game's rules and objectives.

Divide the participants into teams of not more than five people and ask the teams to sit together. Arrange the teams around the room in a circle or square with a little room between them so you can tell them apart. Ask the teams to take about a minute and select a team name.

 Facilitator: Prepare a new flip chart with spaces for each team's name.

Call on the teams, and write their names on the flip chart. Allow enough space to record their scores.

 Facilitator: Display overhead 3.29.

Use overhead 3.29 during the game. After the teams choose a category and you ask the question, mark the question square so everyone can tell it has been played. Now you are ready to play. The lists of questions and answers follow.

Rules for the Conflict Game of Peril

- The objective is to score the most points.
- You score points as a team.
- You can confer with your team members, and you can make a move independently as well.
- Use your voice as a buzzer to signal that you want to make a guess—make a sound like "bagh."
- Pick a category and then a question for ten, twenty, thirty, or forty points.

3.27

Rules for the Conflict Game of Peril (Cont.)

- The group that answers correctly gets the points and makes the next selection.
- Any person can buzz and answer the question, but only after the question is read completely.
- No points are lost for a wrong guess, but the team must wait to go again until all other teams have had a turn.

3.28

Categories in The Conflict Game of Peril

Conflict styles and archetypes	10	20	30	40
Integrative conflict management	10	20	30	40
Negotiation preparation	10	20	30	40
Communication skills	10	20	30	40

3.29

Conflict Styles and Archetypes

10 points

Question: Name the two axes on the conflict management styles grid.

Answer: Concern for self and concern for others.

20 points

Question: Name the five conflict styles.

Answer: Avoidance, accommodation, compromise, competition, and collaboration.

30 points

Question: What four archetypes were given for dealing with conflict?

Answer: Warrior, saint, teacher, student.

40 points

Question: What is the difference between compromise and collaboration?

Answer: In compromise each partner gets half of what they want; in collaboration each party wins. (Also acceptable—in collaboration a creative solution is found that serves the interests of both parties; win-lose versus win-win; zero-sum versus nonzero-sum game.)

Integrative Conflict Management

10 points

Question: Explain what is meant by a "zero-sum game."

Answer: One party wins, + 1; one party loses, - 1; and the sum is zero.

20 points

Question: Give the formula for compromise.

Answer: $+ \frac{1}{2} - \frac{1}{2} + \frac{1}{2} - \frac{1}{2} = 0$.

30 points

Question: Describe the difference in communication between distributive and integrative conflict management.

Answer: Distributive—withholding information, deception, seeking information; integrative—open communication, information sharing, shared inquiry.

40 points

Question: Give the definition of conflict from the opening of the session.

Answer: The major concepts in italics must be included: Conflict occurs when *interdependent* people pursue *goals and values* and *perceive interference* from one another.

Negotiation Preparation

10 points

Question: In preparing for negotiation, what is the advantage of the "best option other than negotiating"?

Answer: This option gives you the power to leave the negotiation—that is, you do not have to settle for less than your best option other than negotiating.

20 points

Question: Name the five areas on the negotiation preparation worksheet.

Answer: Your interests, the other person's interests, creative options, your best option other than negotiating, and the least you will live with.

30 points

Question: Give two methods for finding creative solutions.

Answer: Any two of the following—generate a climate for creativity and new possibilities; brainstorm; expand the possibilities; seek superordinate goals.

40 points

Question: What were at least three of the guidelines given in "What to Do before the Conversation"?

Answer: The guidelines given were:

- Cool off.

- Find a time convenient to both parties.

- Prepare using the worksheet.

- Set a positive tone.

- Review the characteristics of supportive and defensive climates and the communication skills in this workshop.

Communication Skills

10 points

Question: Provide an example of an I statement.

Answer: The I statement must begin with "I [plus verb]" and be stated in a way that does not encourage defensiveness.

20 points

Question: What are the steps in formatting an I statement? Name at least three.

Answer: The four steps are ownership, problem, intermediate goal, and final goal.

30 points

Question: What is the major benefit of confirming the other person's point of view?

Answer: Name at least one:

- It reduces defensiveness.

- He or she will listen better to your interests.

- It helps you reconnect. The person feels understood, and you can continue the negotiation.

40 points

Question: Give at least three guidelines for confirming the other person's point of view.

Answer: The guidelines given were:

- Slow down the process.

- Imagine how the other person feels and thinks.

- Ask a constructive question for more information.

- Confirm the person's experience.

- Offer to help.

- Continue to negotiate.

Keep the game educational, lighthearted, and fun. You must think on your feet when conducting this game. Try to be fair and consistent. Give the teams credit if they are 80 percent right. Pay close attention to who buzzes first. Do not let people answer who buzz before you finish asking the question. Remember to mark each question square on the overhead as you ask it so everyone can see it is done.

After you finish all of the questions, tally the scores. Give the prizes to the winning team and consolation prizes to everyone else. Transition to the last segment.

Development Plan

Time for segment: 15 minutes

 Facilitator: Ask participants to complete activity 3.7 in their workbooks.

This activity represents the participants' personal plan for ongoing development in conflict management. Review the workbook activity with them. Give them eight minutes to complete it. The workbook provides space for two goals. Ask participants to complete at least one.

Exercise 3.6. Share Plan with a Partner

If time allows, invite the participants to share one of their plans with a partner. Give them five minutes for this activity, and alert them at halftime so the partners get a chance to explain their plans.

SUMMARY

Time for segment: 5 minutes

 Facilitator: Show overheads 3.30 and 3.31.

Module Agenda • Total time: Four hours • Conflict styles and strategies • Integrative conflict management • Negotiation planning • Communication skills and cases ——————— 3.30 © 2001 Joshua D. Guilar	*Module Agenda (Cont.)* • Break: Fifteen Minutes • Communication skills and cases (continued) • Third-party intervention • Development in conflict management ——————— 3.31 © 2001 Joshua D. Guilar

DEVELOPMENT PLAN FOR CONFLICT MANAGEMENT

Reflect on the skills you have studied in this session. Answer the question, What development in conflict management would be a breakthrough for me? You are working with the first step in the development process—awareness. Brainstorm and jot your answers in the space below. All possibilities are good possibilities.

Possible development areas:

Next select an area for development. Consider the following criteria.

- The development goal would be a *breakthrough* for you in your relationships with others.

- The goal is *concrete*—that is, you and others could observe whether you perform the behavior.

- The *results* of the goal are observable. For example, if you perform the behavior well, you will observe its positive effects in others and in your relationships.

- You select the goal freely and feel an *internal commitment* toward this goal.

Write your goal on the following form.

Development Area 1

Your commitment to development in conflict management:

_____

_____

_____

_____

Why you have selected this goal:

_____

_____

_____

_____

How you will accomplish this goal (include research, plans, behaviors):

_____

_____

_____

_____

Others who can help you accomplish this goal:

_____

_____

_____

_____

How you will follow up and know if you are successful:

_____

_____

_____

Development Area 2

Your commitment to development in conflict management:

_____

_____

_____

_____

Why you have selected this goal:

_____

_____

_____

_____

How you will accomplish this goal (include research, plans, behaviors):

_____

_____

_____

_____

Others who can help you accomplish this goal:

_____

_____

_____

_____

How you will follow up and know if you are successful:

_____

_____

_____

_____

The overheads outline the session's objectives. Use this material to organize a review of the main skills taught in the module. Go around the room and ask each person what he or she learned in the session. Allow time for discussion.

> The way we manage conflict says a great deal about our temperaments, or the way we relate to other people. Self-knowledge about our avoidance, assertiveness, or aggressiveness in conflict management is an asset. Of the three styles, assertiveness takes the most skill and tends to be the most productive.
>
> In this session, we have created a toolbox of skills and strategies to use for our own benefit and for us to help others. Use these skills to achieve the goals outlined on your development plan. The way to use conflict as a source of learning and productivity is through your continuous development with these tools.

NOTES

1. R. Fisher and D. Ertel, *Getting Ready to Negotiate: The Getting to Yes Workbook* (New York: Penguin Books, 1995); W. Ury, *The Third Side: Why We Fight and How We Can Stop* (New York: Penguin 2000); R. J. Lewicki, D. M. Saunders, and J. W. Minton, *Negotiation,* 3d ed. (Boston: McGraw-Hill, 1998); R. Lulofs and D. Cahn, *Conflict: From Theory to Action* (Needham Heights, MA: Allyn & Bacon, 2000); and W. Ury, *Getting Past No: Negotiating Your Way from Confrontation to Cooperation* (New York: Bantam Books, 1993).
2. M. Buber, *Elements of the Interhuman,* ed. Maurice Friedman, trans. R. Smith, as appears in J. Steward, Ed. *Bridges Not Walls, 7th ed.* (New York: McGraw-Hill 1999), pp. 579–590.
3. W. Ury, *Getting Past No.*
4. Carl Rogers, *A Way of Being,* as appears in J. Steward, Ed., *Bridges Not Walls, 7th ed.* (New York: McGraw-Hill 1999), pp. 566–573.
5. W. Ury, *Getting Past No.*
6. Fisher, Ury, and Patton, *Getting to Yes.*

CONVERSATIONS FOR COORDINATING ACTION

INTRODUCTION

Communication is the most important feature of contemporary work. With the rise of information technology and the service industry, communication now dominates the day-to-day activity of the workplace. Through communication we find our jobs, get hired, establish our networks, and accomplish our goals.

In this module we will focus on developing the interpersonal skills we need to connect with people and to establish mutual commitments in order to get results. These skills build on all the previous work we have done with listening, assertiveness, and conflict management. This session is the workshop's capstone. In keeping with organizational objectives, the goal of training in interpersonal communication is to coordinate action and achieve results.

INSTRUCTOR PREPARATION

Resources for instructor development are in chapter 6. Study these references before teaching this session. The first three workbook activities in this session all have to do with time—the relationship between the past, present, and future of our work lives. A good resource for this work is Robert Grudin's *Time and the Art of Living.*[1]

✓ Materials

Assemble these materials before the session:

- ❏ Overhead transparencies or slide show with appropriate equipment
- ❏ Two flip-chart pads on easels with markers
- ❏ Flip-chart pages prepared with content and titles
- ❏ Participant workbooks
- ❏ Trainer's workshop guide

✓ Checklist

Check the facility carefully before the participants arrive:

- ❏ Does the equipment work?
- ❏ Are tables and chairs arranged appropriately?
- ❏ Are windows, doors, and lighting comfortable?
- ❏ If the break includes refreshments, are they set up?
- ❏ Do you know the location of rest rooms and telephones?
- ❏ Do you know the numbers and contacts for emergency assistance?
- ❏ Are the flip charts set up with markers?
- ❏ Are name tents available with markers?

 Facilitator: Display overhead 4.1 as participants arrive. Full-size overheads are in appendix B.

Conversations for Coordinating Action

Powerful skills for aligning commitment and
accomplishing extraordinary results

4.1   © 2001 Joshua D. Guilar

Scope and Sequence

This session completes the workshop by integrating the skills learned in previous modules with interpersonal collaboration. The session begins with the participants assessing their own accountability and commitments at work.

Next, participants explore skills for designing conversations that align their commitments with others toward action and results. The session organizes these conversations according to their purposes:

- Connection and relationship
- Cocreation

- Partnership and alignment
- Action and accountability
- Learning and completion

The last purpose—conversations for learning and completion—leads to the session's final segment in which you ask the participants to write their final personal development plan and to commit to doing follow-up work after the workshop. The workshop ends with your wind-up presentation.

LECTURE NOTES: CONVERSATIONS FOR COORDINATING ACTION

Total time: **4 hours**
Midpoint break: **15 minutes**

Introduction

Time for segment: 15 minutes

As always, prepare your introduction carefully to engage the participants and set the tone for the session. Inform the participants that they will complete their work from the first three sessions—work in listening, assertiveness, and conflict management—by building a final set of skills for aligning commitment, coordinating action, and getting positive results in organizations.

Exercise 4.1. Gauging the Commitment of Participants

 Facilitator: Display overhead 4.2.

Introduce the workshop and review the three questions posed in overhead 4.2. Your purpose is twofold: to meet the session's key objectives—to encourage the participants to reflect on their commitments and accountability in the workshop and

---

Three Questions

- What do you plan to contribute in this workshop today?
- How accountable are you for your experience in this group today?
- How much responsibility do you plan to take for the experience of others in this group?

4.2   © 2001 Joshua D. Guilar

---

in general—and to get them fully engaged in the workshop.

Explain the exercise to the participants. Have them rate their responses to the overhead's three questions on a scale of one to five, with one representing very low and five representing very high. Ask them to write their ratings in the extra space in their workbooks.

After they record their ratings, ask for a show of hands. Ask, "For the first question, how many people wrote one?" Acknowledge their response and proceed with the other ratings and questions. Your want to get them thinking about their commitment and accountability. There are no right or wrong answers.

Summarize the activity by stating the session's purpose: We will build powerful communication skills for action, and coordinating that action requires establishing shared commitments. Often in organizations, people become passive and noncommittal because they believe accountability rests with others. They blame poor systems, inadequate leadership, staid organizational culture, and a lack of resources for their situations. *Accountability,* however, begins with being responsible for our own commitments and our immediate relationships.

 Facilitator: Display and read overheads 4.3 and 4.4.

 Facilitator: Next show overhead 4.5.

Explain that these conversations for action have five purposes that combine for effectiveness in organizations. Then read the five purposes out loud to the group.

Personal Commitments

Time for segment: 30 minutes

Aligning your commitment with others begins with understanding your own commitments. Commitment is powerful. To be committed to a project and its completion is challenging and fulfilling, particularly when working with others who are just as devoted. Today the need for such coordinated action is the major feature of work in most organizations.

Interpersonal communication involves *intra*personal communication. *Intrapersonal communication* involves the self and what goes on inside you, the person. Intrapersonal communication is our thinking, feeling, motivation, and intentions. Our first step in aligning our actions and efforts with others is to understand ourselves, especially our commitments and our strengths. Workbook activity 4.1 will help you focus on your commitments.

Module Agenda

- Total time: Four hours
- Introduction
- Personal commitments
- Conversations for action
- Conversations for relationship and connection
- Conversations for cocreation
- Break: Fifteen minutes

4.3

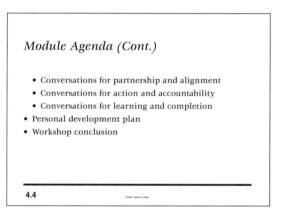

Module Agenda (Cont.)

- Conversations for partnership and alignment
- Conversations for action and accountability
- Conversations for learning and completion
- Personal development plan
- Workshop conclusion

4.4

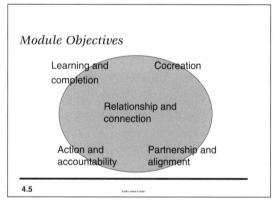

Module Objectives

Learning and completion

Cocreation

Relationship and connection

Action and accountability

Partnership and alignment

4.5

Each of our lives forms a pattern or a story. If we take time out to examine them, we can see these patterns within the history of our work experiences. In this activity, recall your major jobs, projects, and work accomplishments. Overhead 4.6 shows an example of this activity.

 Facilitator: Display overhead 4.6 and instruct everyone to turn to workbook activity 4.1.

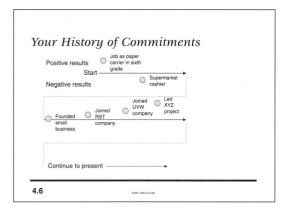

Explain the overhead. Instruct the participants to turn to workbook activity 4.1, and read the instructions with them. As they trace their work history and experience, they will see the trends and patterns in their work lives. Circulate, and help them with the activity.

As the first participants complete their time lines, ask them to look for any patterns. Instruct them to complete part 2, which asks for the themes they found in their time lines. They need to consider what is important and redundant in their history of commitment. When they are all finished, ask them about the patterns in their time lines. Discuss these patterns with the participants. Wind up the discussion by relating their work histories to the present and to the future.

Understanding our past gives us insight into our strengths and into what we can accomplish in the future. Your time line shows your commitments from the past and how you felt about those experiences. In the next activity, you will assess your current commitments, or what is on your plate at present.

 Facilitator: Instruct everyone to turn to workbook activity 4.2.

Instruct the participants to brainstorm a list of their commitments associated with their current jobs. They do not have to list them in rank order. Because the commitments for each job tend to differ, encourage each person to do this work individually.

In step 2 the participants write down the work commitments they would like to make in the coming year. Emphasize that our vision of the future helps us fashion our commitments in the present. If we plan, we can create our future.

YOUR HISTORY OF COMMITMENTS

On the time line below, draw a circle and label the jobs, projects, and major commitments from your work life. Begin with the first job you can remember and proceed to your hopes for the future. If you found a job or project a positive emotional experience, place its circle above the line; if negative, draw it below.

Part 1. Time Line

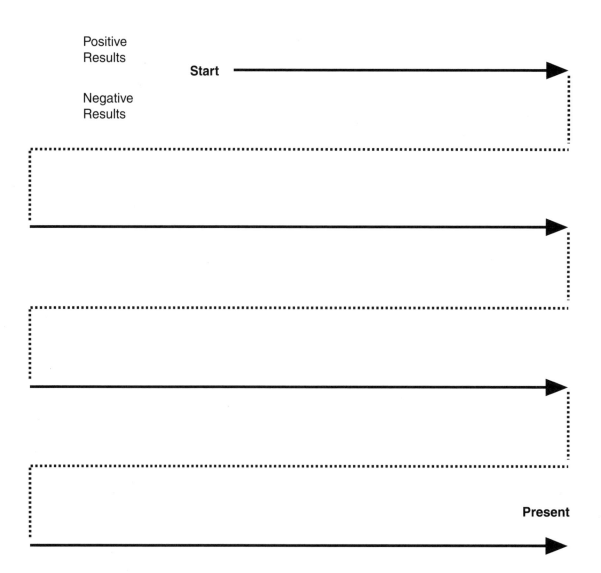

Positive
Results

Start

Negative
Results

Present

Part 2. Themes

Reflect on the trends and patterns you see on your time line. Then in the space below, write the themes you see in your history of work commitments. For example, what are your strengths? Focus on the items above the time line—that is, the projects and jobs you found emotionally positive.

Themes in your work history:

_____

_____

_____

_____

_____

_____

_____

_____

_____

_____

_____

_____

_____

_____

_____

_____

_____

_____

_____

_____

_____

_____

YOUR WORK COMMITMENTS

Step 1. Your Current Commitments

In the space below, brainstorm a list of your current work commitments. You do not have to rank them.

Your present work commitments:
_____

_____

_____

_____

_____

_____

_____

Step 2. New Commitments

Make a list of the additional commitments you would like to make in the coming year.

Commitments you would like to make in the coming year:
_____

_____

_____

_____

_____

_____

_____

Step 3. What Is It Time For?

Finally, given your current commitments and the commitments you would like to make in the coming year, rank order your commitments in the box below. Rank your commitments by answering the question, What is it time for?

Your top work commitments in order of importance:

_____

_____

_____

_____

_____

_____

_____

_____

_____

_____

_____

_____

_____

_____

_____

_____

_____

_____

_____

_____

Remember these commitments. We will return to them later.

Facilitator: Display and read overhead 4.7. Pronounce the name Czelaw Milosz "Cheslof Mewash."

Listen to the following quotes. Maybe these men's words will inspire you to identify your most important commitments.

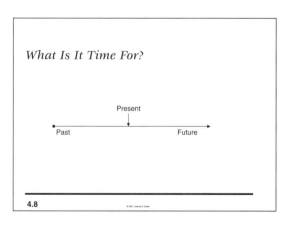

Projects and Commitments

- To undertake a project, as the word's derivation indicates, means to cast an idea out ahead of oneself so that it gains autonomy and is fulfilled not only by the efforts of its originator but, indeed, independently of him as well.

—Czelaw Milosz

4.7

Whatever you can do, or dream you can, begin it. Boldness has genius, power, and magic in it.

—*Goethe*

Without ambition one starts nothing. Without work one accomplishes nothing. The prize will not be sent to you. You have to earn it.

—*Ralph Waldo Emerson*

I am of the opinion that my life belongs to the whole community, and as long as I live it is my privilege to do for it whatever I can.

—*George Bernard Shaw.*

In the third step, they answer the question, What is it time for? In this final step, participants rank order their commitments.

How many of you keep day timers? If you analyzed all of the meetings, projects, and activities you did last year, how much time would you have listed as unproductive? Think about it: How many meetings were a waste of time? How many were actually productive?

Usually, these types of questions help participants focus on the right commitments.

 Facilitator: Show overhead 4.8.

To select the best commitment for us we must first understand our strengths and fulfillment with work as experienced in our past. We also need to figure out how to sustain our fulfillment in the future. We can enhance the effects of our past and future

What Is It Time For?

Present

Past   Future

4.8

experiences through reflection and planning. As Robin Grudin points out,

Only by asserting yourself in time can you achieve functional identity and become in fact what you seem to be . . . Such an assertion is impossible without a plan for personal development which forcefully projects your character into the future.[2]

> As we take control of our experiences and how they shape our self-image and our views of the world, we also recognize that our work has an impact on the world we live in. Think of Bill Gates, a man who is tremendously successful in business because he selected projects that helped shape the way the world works. He certainly focused on the right commitments when he steered his organization to working on the operating systems for PCs and to information sharing.

In step 1, the participants pick the commitment that is most important to them. Everyone has unique criteria. Point out that knowing their own commitments is the first step in coordinating action with others. In the second step the participants identify the people that can help them accomplish their highest-ranked commitment.

 Facilitator: Instruct participants to do workbook activity 4.3.

After the participants finish their lists of commitments, ask them to share their lists in pairs. Let each person take about two minutes to explain their most important commitments to a partner. Circulate and listen to as many pairs as you can.

 ## Training Tip: Action Learning

In the following exercise, the participants identify actual projects in their jobs, and they will use one of these projects as they work through the session's activities. *Action learning* brings the participants' real-life projects into the training room. This personalization helps you engage the participants and helps them transfer what they learn back to the workplace.

Preview: Five Conversations for Coordinating Action

Time for segment: 5 minutes

 Facilitator: Tell a story.

Share a story about someone who pulled together a team to accomplish a great project. Perhaps you have a story from your own work life. If not, you can find many stories in the business literature—for example, Stephen Jobs who pulled together the Macintosh team at Apple. In *Organizing Genius: The Secrets of Creative Collaboration,* Warren Bennis and P. Biederman provide stories about people who accomplished great projects by creating networks of committed people.[3] Remember to relate the story to how things get done in organizations, which is through communication.

RANKING YOUR COMMITMENTS

In the space below, write the highest-ranking work commitment from the last exercise.

Step 1. Your Top Work Commitment

Describe your top work commitment:

_____

_____

_____

_____

_____

Step 2. Those People Who Can Help You

In the space below, write the names of the people who can help you act on your commitment.

Names of partners:

_____

_____

_____

_____

_____

_____

_____

_____

Facilitator: Display and read overhead 4.9.

Conversations for Connection and Relationship

Time for segment: 25 minutes

> ### Five Conversations for Coordinating Action
>
> 1. Relationship and connection
> 2. Cocreation
> 3. Partnership
> 4. Action and accountability
> 5. Learning and completion
>
> _____
>
> 4.9

Contemporary work is mostly communication, and the most successful people establish extensive networks. In this segment we will cover the skills for building connected relationships. Connection is one of several characteristics of relationship such as openness, relative power, or intimacy. Connection in the workplace is the mutual force that makes people want to work and to communicate together.

Our capacity to establish effective work relationships is crucial to our success. Our connection and relationships with others are the most sustainable foundations of our power and enable us to make things happen in our organizations. When we engage in a conversation to establish a relationship, we use deep listening, mutuality, appreciation, and genuine inquiry. Building work relationships involves learning about the private perceptual worlds of others and letting them know that you are supportive and committed to their interests along with those of the organization.

Andrew, for instance, is a manager of a corporate division supplying workers' compensation insurance and consulting for the health care industry. About seventy-five people work in Andy's division; however, some of his most important projects involve collaboration with people who work in other divisions. His success depends on the contribution of people with whom he has no formal authority. Andy's success and his basis for power rest primarily on his ability to connect with others and to create effective and voluntary work relationships.

As Robert Louis Stevenson said, "So long as we love, we serve; so long as we are loved by others, we are indispensable." We all have experienced that connection with other people, but most of us at some point have experienced a feeling of disconnection as well. Picture those coworkers with whom you feel the most disconnected. What contributes to disconnection between people?

Tell the participants that you want their input. Go around the room and call on people, or wait for volunteers.

 Facilitator: Write their ideas on a flip chart, and leave them displayed.

Summarize their responses. What did they emphasize and repeat? What are the themes?

 Facilitator: Create another flip chart, write "Why we connect" across the top, and follow the same process.

Think of someone with whom you coordinate action and with whom you feel connected. What makes you connected? What attracts you to that person? How do you affect that connection? How does the situation affect your perception?

Again collect the participants' responses and record them on the flip chart. Summarize their input.

 Facilitator: Display and review overhead 4.10, which probably lists ideas already generated by the participants. Make connections with the participants' examples as you read the overhead.

Conversations for Connection

Connection	vs.	Disconnection
• Listening for mutuality		• Not listening, self-interested
• Authenticity and trust		• Superficiality and distrust
• Emotional intelligence		• Defensiveness
• Seeing each person as unique		• Stereotyping

4.10   © 2001 Joshua D. Guilar

The overhead summarizes the four distinctions between connection and disconnection. We are now applying the skills we learned in module 1 to effect change in organizations. This session is an opportunity to practice. Remember, learning and improving communication skills require practice. Similar to learning a new language, if you do not use it, you lose it!

 Facilitator: Display overhead 4.11.

Listening For . . .

• Commitments of others
• Opportunities for sincere appreciation
• Mutual interests
• Their concerns
• The listening of others

4.11   © 2001 Joshua D. Guilar

Now we will consider each distinction of connection, beginning with listening. Listening and responding to mutual interests create connection, which is important for coordinating action. Connection persists throughout the five conversations we outlined as conditions for coordinating action with others. Read the overhead. It lists the important things to listen *for* when building a relationship to coordinate action.

The central feature of collaboration in all of its phases is the power of our listening, which is akin to the power of our perception. When we use powerful listening, we connect with others almost immediately, and with time and trust, these relationships deepen into our greatest assets at work.

Authenticity is about how comfortable we feel in our own skins and how forthright and direct we are when we express our experience and interests to others. Authenticity builds trust. Without authenticity we hide our experience and interests, and our superficiality creates mistrust.

Facilitator: Show and read overheads 4.12 and 4.13.

Authenticity can be a little scary. Many people in organizations feel a great pressure to conform; however, the external causes for conformity and superficiality are probably overrated. What makes us superficial is our own fear and lack of courage. Authenticity, which often involves confrontation, does not necessarily involve conflict or punishment. As a matter of fact, authenticity can be rewarding and connect people when used tactfully.

The next feature of relationships and connection is emotional intelligence. *Emotional intelligence* is self-awareness and a form of communication that motivates us to be connected and empathic with others.

> *Authenticity*
>
> • Is saying tactfully what you are experiencing.
> • Reveals others' and your assumptions.
> • Brings resistance to light and provides for breakthroughs.
>
> 4.12

> *Authenticity (Cont.)*
>
> • Provides greater functionality.
> • Is the antidote to being manipulative.
> • Builds trust and relationships.
> • Is the essential courage.
>
> 4.13

Facilitator: Display and read overhead 4.14.

Be prepared to tell a story about emotional intelligence. There are many books on the subject—see, for example, Daniel Goleman's *Emotional Intelligence* or Hendrie Weisinger's *Emotional Intelligence at Work*—but you probably know

> *Emotional Intelligence*
>
> • Requires being aware of emotion as it happens in oneself, others, and the environment.
> • Involves appreciation of oneself and others.
> • Results in self-confidence.
> • Is grace under fire, harmony, and ease in interpersonal relationships.
> • Is a quality of leadership and connection.
>
> 4.14

people who set a great emotional tone for work and for relationship.⁴ Emotional intelligence creates the tone for connection. We are more likely to connect with people who appreciate us. The same is true for others' connection with us. People will connect with us when they feel appreciated. The opposite of emotional intelligence is *emotional defensiveness,* or unconsciously responding to others as if they were a threat.

Transition to the fourth and last feature of conversations for relationship and connection—that of *seeing each person as unique.* This last feature also deals with perception, which helps us distinguish between seeing each person as a unique individual and seeing people as stereotypes.

 Facilitator: Show and read overhead 4.15.

Seeing Each Person as Unique

Problem	Solution
• Think and deal on the basis of inferences.	• Think and deal on the basis of facts.
• Stereotype based on cultural and social backgrounds.	• See each person as unique.
• Use polarizing language.	• Use language accurately.

4.15

We often disconnect with people as a result of our intrapersonal communication, or what goes on in our own heads. The human mind is a beautiful thing, but some of its natural processes create problems in human relationships. For instance, consider inferential thinking and stereotyping. *Inferential thinking* consists of making leaps from the known to the unknown. We discover a little bit about something or somebody, and then we make a leap and guess that we know much more. We act as if our inferences are facts. Stereotyping is an example.

Here is a simile to help explain this process. Our minds work like the hard drive of a computer. In it we build directories or categories into which we put our files. Our relationships are similar—we put people into categories. We start a file for each new person we meet. The problem comes when we perceive people and interact with them as if they were like the files in our filing system. We forget they are people with unique characteristics. Our filing system corrupts the relationship away from reality, which is always more complex and up-to-date than our filing system allows.

Let's say someone new transfers to your department at work. He passes your desk in a hurry and does not say anything. In your file on him you put a note marked "unfriendly." Then at the watercooler later in the day, a coworker remarks, "That new person hasn't said a word to me. He sure is unfriendly." So you put another note in your file marked "unfriendly for sure." Now you are on the alert for more similar information, but you do not look for disconfirming or contrary information.

To rectify such inferential thinking, recognize stereotyping for what it is and seek out the facts. If you approach the new worker and connect with him, you can find out what is really going on. Perhaps he's shy, or he's under a great deal of stress and is temporarily distracted. Get the facts, and keep your files to a minimum.

Inferential thinking and stereotyping are big problems in intercultural communication. The same problems we have in any relationship tend to be exacerbated when we interact with people who are racially, socially, or otherwise unfamiliar to us. The more unfamiliar they are, the more likely we will stereotype. Seeing each person as unique overcomes problems of stereotyping and inferential thinking that tend to affect all relationships but are particular problems in intercultural contexts.

Disconnection occurs when we stereotype. The more we treat people superficially as fitting into categories, the more we objectify them and the less we personally relate to them. Our language betrays our objectification and polarizes us from those with whom we could collaborate. Examples of such language include sexist language, stereotypes, and political, religious, social, and cultural labels.

The last item on the overhead is polarizing language. Polarizing language divides life into extremes—for example, are you for or against the proposal? A less polarizing question would be, What are your views on supporting the proposal? Another example of polarizing language is to say something is always (or never) true. In fact, there is very little that is always or never true. To say someone is always slow to commit is probably not true. We index our language when we give a particular time or condition. For example, last year John was slow to commit to the supply chain project. This is far different from saying that John is always slow to commit. Sexist and racist language are extreme examples of polarization.

The relationship-connection model has four features—listening, authenticity, emotional intelligence, and seeing others as unique. Communication at work has two dimensions—the *social dimension* of relationships and the *task dimension,* which is the material content of our work. Both aspects are important. While attending to your task dimensions, remember your commitments to focus on establishing, maintaining, and deepening your relationships.

Conversations for Cocreation

Time for segment: 25 minutes

People are never so involved as when they help create something. This generative process motivates them. In the best teams and relationships, interaction is a creative faculty. Think about your conversations at work. How many of them are creative? Who have you worked with who generates creative conversations? What is he or she like?

Facilitator: Ask the group for stories about people who generate creative conversations at work. Acknowledge their stories, and probe for more information, relating their answers to the prior conversation on relationships.

Creative conversations build on strong, positive relationships. The emotional tone of the relationship provides the inspiration for creativity.

Creativity is one of a few key tools we need to live life successfully.[5] In this segment we will first define creativity, and then we will explore means to solicit creative responses in an exercise.

 Facilitator: Show overheads 4.16 and 4.17, and explain their points.

Interpersonal creativity occurs when people generate something new and useful through conversations. Who here is creative?

 Facilitator: Acknowledge those who respond positively. Then encourage those people who do not answer to recognize their creativity also.

We do not have to be Picasso or Einstein to be considered creative. We all can be creative in everyday ways—in arranging flowers in a vase, in seeing things differently than we have seen them before, or in appreciating something or somebody for the first time. We are all creative, and we can develop this capacity further.

Think back to my earlier question, Do you know someone at work who is creative? Think about that coworker. I bet that this person creates open, supportive, and playful relationships with others.

As with the other skills in these workshops, we have tools to help us develop our creativity. Developing our creativity is like tending a garden. First we have to prepare the earth or open up our minds to possibilities. Then we need to plant new seeds or ideas, friendships, and projects. And we have tools at our disposal to prompt growth, or creativity.

One such tool is *unlearning.* As educator Neil Postman once said, "Children enter school as question marks and leave as periods."[6] Societal influences can make us quite submissive—that is, to see only one right answer, to conform, to not dare to take risks, to hate ourselves for our mistakes, and to refrain from reflecting on our creativity and from bringing creativity into our conversations with others.

Interpersonal Creativity. . .

Conversations for Cocreation
- Generates something new and useful through conversations between people.
- Is something we all can experience.
- Requires openness, support, and playfulness.

4.16

Interpersonal Creativity (Cont.)

- Comes through using tools:
  - Unlearning
  - Asking "what if" questions
  - Using associations and metaphors
  - Inviting diversity
  - Learning from mistakes
- Is fulfilled when we take a new idea into action with others.

4.17

A conversation for creativity, however, is about becoming open to possibilities. This openness is the opposite of already knowing all the answers. As the philosopher Søren Kierkegaard said, "If I were to wish for anything, [it would be] the passionate sense of the potential."

Creativity comes from within. Now here is a great question.

 Facilitator: Show overhead 4.18. Ask the trainees what it means.

 Facilitator: Next, switch to overhead 4.19.

Creativity is the source of all humor and an indispensable element in living life well. Notice that "aha!"—the sound of discovery—and "ha-ha!" are similar.

Tell a brief story from your own experience to illustrate this point. Next, explain the examples found in overheads 4.20 and 4.21, and help the participants gain a sense of how creativity pervades our decisions every day.

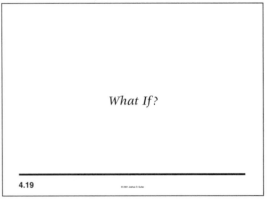

 Facilitator: Show and read overheads 4.20 and 4.21.

Living What If . . .

Problem: Recently your section doubled in size to 500 people. However, your department, which is a support function, has stayed the same size. You are swamped.

Creative Solutions:
• Have a brainstorming session.
• Seize this opportunity to lead change.

4.20

Living What If (Cont.)

• Redesign the department.
• Ask for more employees.
• Design protocols to prioritize work.
• Outsource to venders.
• Move to the Virgin Islands.

4.21

Exercise 4.2. The What If Exercise

In the "what if" exercise, you work in pairs and ask the question about a specific problem. First, write down a list of problems—any problems are fine—you have at work. Just brainstorm a list and write as many as possible. Let your creative juices flow.

Next, get a partner. Together, review your lists of problems and select one that both partners have in common or one you both wish to work with. Then take turns asking, "What if?" Share as many answers to the question as possible, and write them down. You have five minutes.

After five minutes, debrief. Ask for volunteers to share their lists. Ask everyone in the room what they learned and experienced.

Creativity Killers

Conversations for creativity focus on speculation and possibility. Their tone includes humor, supportiveness, openness, and passion. We would have greater creativity in our respective organizations if it were not for creativity killers.

Tell a story about how creativity can be stifled in organizations. For instance, the Eastman Kodak company rejected an inventor's first proposal for photocopying technology, and Steve Wozniak, a coinventor of the personal computer, once presented the idea for the PC to his research and development (R&D) manager at a major American corporation, but the manager said no. Some people are just too shortsighted to be managers. Use an example of a creativity killer from your own experience.

 Facilitator: Show overheads 4.22 and 23.

Explain that conversations have to be designed for creativity, because most people tend to see the future as the perpetuation of the past—that is, they do not look beyond their own past experience or entertain other possibilities. Such tools as brainstorming increase creativity and possibilities because they eliminate the tendency to rush to evaluation and decision making.

Summarize conversations for creativity:

• Everyone is creative and can develop these capacities further by studying and using the tools.

• Use such tools as the what-if question, association, and humor every day.

• Create with others interpersonally and look for opportunities for creativity.

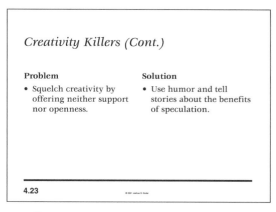

Creativity Killers

Problem	Solution
• Dismisses as impossible, or already knows it will not work here; sees future as continuation of past.	• Explore the possibility by reframing conversation.
• Has no time for creativity—just decision and evaluation.	• Make time and ground rules for creativity in the conversation.

4.22

Creativity Killers (Cont.)

Problem	Solution
• Squelch creativity by offering neither support nor openness.	• Use humor and tell stories about the benefits of speculation.

4.23

- Identify and reframe conversations when people undermine new possibilities.
- Be open to new possibilities for yourself and for others.

Conversations for creativity require us to speculate together, to value diverse points of view, and to value the unknown and the possible. Innovation is crucial for the enduring success of many organizations. Look at leading-edge high-technology firms and you'll see they often generate the majority of their revenues from products they introduced within the last two years.

Midpoint Break

Time for break: 15 minutes

Clearly state your expectations about starting on time after the break. The topic when they return is conversations for partnership and alignment.

Conversations for Partnership and Alignment

Time for segment: 30 minutes

> Partnership builds on the first two conversations. *Partnership* builds on trusting relationships and on sharing the creation of projects. Conversations for partnership focus on mutuality, or the interests and commitments both parties share.
>
> Speaking of commitments, let's return to workbook activity 4.3 in which you ranked your commitments. I want you to review your top commitment and to keep it in mind as we move forward.
>
> Today more than ever before we get things done through partnerships. We are interdependent, and the people we rely on to get things done often do not report to us—that is, we have no formal authority over them.
>
> Productive people in organizations rely on networks of relationships. The more effective people have larger networks. I know one manager who has a working relationship with more than 200 people in her organization—in different departments, functions, and levels. She can call on any of these people to make things happen, and she is one of the most effective people I know.

> *Facilitator: Draw a simple hub network on a flip chart. Identify the different roles—hub, member, and liaison. The hub is the person in a group through whom information passes. He or she is the center of communication and relationship. A liaison is someone who is not a member of the group but whose role is to form an information channel with other groups and individuals.*

For an explanation of networks see Miller (1999). Have participants think about a network in a television show, such as *Seinfeld.*[7] Ask for a volunteer to

YOUR NETWORK OF PARTNERS

Diagram below your network of partners. Use the list you made in workbook activity 4.3. The instructor will show you an example on an overhead.

Your Resource Network

draw the network of relationships in the sitcom and to label the different roles. When the trainee is finished, thank him or her.

 Facilitator: Show them the example on overhead 4.24.

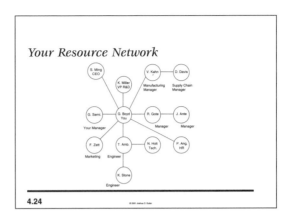

Your Resource Network

4.24

Relate the concept of networks back to their highest-ranked commitment at work and transition to workbook activity 4.4.

In this activity, the trainees identify the people and the network they need to take action on their highest-ranked commitment. Ask them to return to workbook activity 4.3 and to review step 1—their commitment—and step 2, in which they listed their potential partners and all of those people who can help them achieve their goal.

In this activity, the participants draw their networks.

As the participants finish their networks, ask them to plan the conversations that they need to have with the partners identified in these networks. When all of them are finished, summarize the activity by reminding them of the following information.

You can use this network to identify the conversations you need to have before you can move forward with your project. Ideas, commitments, and projects are great, but we have to remember the question, What is it time for? What project is actionable in this organization at this time? To answer these questions you need to discuss these issues with your partners before you move into action. Your partners need to help you shape the project so they can support it.

 Facilitator: Show overheads 4.25 and 4.26, and read each one out loud.

Interpersonal Partnership

- Occurs through conversation before taking action
- Determines the timeliness of actions, commitments, and projects
- Involves listening for commitments, politics, information, and resistance
- Encounters barriers—interpersonal, functional, and hierarchical
- Is based on cooperation, mutuality, and shared interests

4.25

Interpersonal Partnership (Cont.)

- Helps shape the project and its implementation.
- Involves trading on:
  - Your reputation for getting things done
  - Reciprocity—I help you; you help me
  - Alliances and connections
  - Position and assets
  - Diplomatic and interpersonal skills

4.26

Explain the points on the overheads. Two good resources about this type of conversation are *The Change Masters* by Rosebeth Moss Kanter and the Robert Kaplan article, "Trade Routes: The Manager's Network of Relationships."[8] Tell a story about someone who went ahead with a project before establishing any partnerships, which is often disastrous. For example, I know an engineer who had a great idea for a process improvement. He conceived the idea, developed it, and then tried to implement it. During implementation he found that no one was interested. Except for its educational value, his efforts were wasted.

Concerning the fourth point on the overhead—barriers—one of the most significant barriers is establishing partnerships with senior managers in other departments. Ask the participants if they have succeeding in making such alliances and to share their stories. Be prepared with one of your own, also.

> The last point on the overhead is about trading, which, in a very real sense, is how things are accomplished in organizations. Trading varies by level. The top of an organization often exchanges good performers and job openings. Information is usually the currency of exchange in the lower levels. Even if you do not have much power yet, you can trade on recognition and develop connections. For example, you can give recognition to a potential partner by asking him or her for advice. The partner gets the social satisfaction of helping you. The good news is that you can form networks fairly quickly and naturally. At the same time, expanding your network takes conscious attention.
>
> We are interdependent. In a conversation for partnership we test an idea for workability and for usefulness. Partnership building involves getting input from others. Competent partnership builders involve key stakeholders, who, in turn, help shape the idea so it is actionable in the organization. For instance, a human performance technologist designing a training program aimed at improving the performance of a manufacturing unit should involve all of the stakeholders—the management, team members, and professional partners—early in the process.

 Facilitator: Transition to the next exercise.

Exercise 4.3. Conversations for Partnership

In this exercise, trainees form into pairs to practice a conversation for partnership, with each partner taking a turn. In turn, the trainees set up hypothetical conversations with their partners. Selecting a commitment or project they have at work, they direct their partners to take a particular role. For example: "I would like you to take the role of the CEO, and I am going to have a conversation with you about my product development project." Both partners have to improvise a conversation. Debrief the conversations. Ask the participants, "How well did this work as a conversation for partnership? Why?" Then have the partners switch roles and repeat the exercise.

> Work in organizations is more interdependent than ever before. Organizations increasingly rely on cross-functional cooperation and exter-

nal alliances. Your success relies on your ability to create an extensive network of relationships and your ability to get things done without formal authority.

 Facilitator: Transition to the next topic, which is conversations for action and accountability.

Conversations for Action and Accountability
Time for segment: 20 minutes

Coordinating action can be simple and straightforward, but often it is not. When was the last time you thought someone had promised to do something for you, and you were surprised when it did not happen? How quickly do people return your e-mail or phone messages? What is the level of accountability in your organization?

Conversations for action build on the prior three conversations—for connection and relationships, for creativity, and for partnership and alignment. If you have a connected relationship with partners who have created the idea with you and been involved in shaping its implementation, you have a strong foundation for coordinating action with them.

Conversations for coordinating action are simple, but we have to pay close attention. *A conversation for coordinating action includes making people accountable for their commitments.* This process means managers must make clear requests and promises and follow up on them. Many managers complain that, although they give directions, their people do not produce or miss their deadlines. The root of this problem is found either in the vagueness of the directions or in the people's lack of accountability. Project leaders need to ensure that others understand the requests and to hold others accountable for their promises. In an effective conversation for action, a manager can help move a project to successful completion or to appropriate reformation.

 Facilitator: Show and read overheads 4.27 and 4.28.

Action and Accountability

- Requests that clarify:
  - *Who* is going to do
  - *What*, by
  - *When*, according to
  - *Which* conditions of satisfaction

4.27   © 2001 Joshua O. Gutin

Action and Accountability (Cont.)

- Promises that hold:
  - Negotiated and voluntary participation
  - Internal commitment
  - Accountability
- Declarations that:
  - Identify breakdowns.
  - Clear away resistance and confusion.

4.28   © 2001 Joshua O. Gutin

Conversations for action and accountability are best understood through the knowledge of *speech acts*.[9] A speech act is a unit of language that expresses a certain meaning and intention. Examples are declarations, questions, commands, requests, and promises. Requests and promises are particularly important for coordinating action because they identify agreement and accountability with cooperation. The major idea is that organizations are networks of commitments, which are coordinated through conversations. Conversational messages have particular purposes—requests, promises, and declarations—that are important in coordinating commitments. As a project runs its course, breakdowns will occur where problems arise. The conversation's design should anticipate these breakdowns as far ahead as possible, and the conversation ought to include accountability to identify and renegotiate terms quickly as breakdowns occur.

 Facilitator: Be prepared. Develop stories and questions to accompany your lectures.

This portion of the lesson is mostly lecture, so be prepared with stories and questions to engage the participants. Prepare a story about a lack of accountability and another about great accountability. Ask the participants if their projects have had any breakdowns lately.

Encourage the participants to use the action and accountability model when making requests. They should ask themselves, "When I made the request, did I include *when* it was due? Did I specify my conditions of satisfaction?" Your *conditions of satisfaction* ought to be specific and verified by a *double interact*. In this process, you follow three steps to ensure that your request is completely understood:

1. The requesting partner specifies the conditions.
2. The second partner agrees to each detail.
3. The first partner confirms the understanding.

You can prepare a role-play about the double interact process. Here is an example: Ask for a volunteer to role-play the interaction involved in a work request. Direct the volunteer to take the role of complying with your request. Make the tone lighthearted and the interaction informative. You play an internal customer who is requesting work from a graphics department in your organization. You need overhead transparencies made for a presentation. You have in your hand the notes that you want made into overheads. Example dialogue follows.

Who will do what?

Requestor: "I would like to request your help with a project. I need overhead transparencies made for a presentation." [Show the respondent your notes.]

Respondent: "Sure thing. I have to go now. I'll see you later." [The respondent takes the notes and turns to go.]

Requestor: "Wait. I need more time to complete this conversation."

When?

Respondent: "Okay."

Requestor: "I need to know by what date you can complete this assignment."

Respondent: "I can get it to you by Tuesday of next week."

Requestor: "Thanks. That would be [provide the exact date.] That will give me enough time to practice before the presentation. But I need the transparencies no later than [exact date], or I will not have enough time to practice."

Respondent: "I understand."

Conditions of Satisfaction

Requestor: "Please take a look at the notes, and let me know if you have any questions."

Respondent: [The respondent looks at the notes] "No, everything looks very clear to me."

Requestor: "Will you use the company template and logo?"

Respondent: "Yes."

Requestor: "So the overheads will be printed on transparencies, put in sleeves, and placed in a binder with the company logo."

Respondent: "Right. If I find any small corrections or typos, can you correct those tomorrow morning, Wednesday?"

Requestor: "Yes. Will you also give me the transparency file on a floppy disk next Tuesday?"

Respondent: "No problem."

Requestor: "Do you have any questions for me?"

Respondent: "No."

Requestor: "I appreciate your help. This presentation is very important for me and for our operation."

Respondent: "You are welcome."

 Facilitator: Thank the person who helped you with the role-play. Debrief the dialogue. What observations did the volunteer have? And what about the rest of the group?

Declarations are speech acts that formally pronounce something as being a reality. One example is a cleric announcing a couple is married. Another example would be a vice-president of manufacturing declaring a breakdown in his department's relationship with R&D, saying R&D's new products are poorly designed for manufacturing. His declaration leads to an exploration of problems, solutions, and future commitments shared between manufacturing and R&D.

In sum, coordinating action is how things get done in organizations. We accomplish our goals through conversations and assigning accountability. Likewise, we can increase the accountability in our relationships through improving requests, promises, and declarations.

Conversations for Learning and Completion
Time for segment: 35 minutes

There is a great deal of action in organizations, but not all of it yields results. There are numerous relationships in organizations, but not all of them are productive. Many projects are started, but some are not completed—and yet no conversation follows their abandonment. Do these sound like understatements?

Do we learn from the projects we abandon? Do we learn from the relationships that don't work? Do we learn from our successes and our mistakes?

Neil Goldschmidt, the former U.S. Secretary of Transportation, was once asked about the failure of a high-speed rail system, the San Francisco Bay Area BART system. Goldschmidt said,

It's gotten too fashionable around the country to beat up on BART and not give credit to the vision that put this system in place. We have learned from BART. The lessons were put to use in Washington, in Atlanta, in Buffalo, and other cities where we've built mass transit systems. One of the lessons is not to build a system like BART.[10]

Conversations for learning involve explorations about:

• Who should be appreciated for their contributions, commitment, accomplishments, and even their mistakes?

• What did we learn—including personal, interpersonal, team, and organizational learning—that we can improve on next time?

• What did we learn that we can share with others who have similar missions?

• How can people lower their defenses and learn together in their everyday work and relationships?

While various authors have popularized organizational learning, its practice is often misunderstood.[11] It is not about training, although training can help organizational learning.

According to V. Marsick and K. Watkins, *organizational learning* "speaks to the collective capacity of a company to respond effectively to a rapidly changing turbulent environment by more effectively fostering, capturing, and sharing learning to reap the benefit of what people know so as to improve performance."[12] Organizational learning is shared learning about work. It focuses particularly on people learning through communication at work. Learning means alternating between action and reflection.

The world that we have made as a result of the level of thinking that we have done thus far creates problems that we cannot solve at the same level at which we created them.

—Albert Einstein

A *conversation for learning* involves people taking time to talk about the process of learning itself. Excellent times for this learning are during a project at review time, or at the end of the project in the debrief. Good questions to ask are: Who deserves appreciation? What have we learned? What have we learned that would be useful to others? What could we improve? Where could we develop further? What are we pretending *not* to know? What are we not talking about that we should be?

A conversation for learning is a dialogue that requires sufficient trust and openness. Often, involving the group leaders and members in open communication is a first step.

Dialogue is a discipline of collective thinking and inquiry, a process for transforming the quality of conversation, and, in particular, the thinking that lies beneath it.

—Bill Isaacs

But where dialogue is fulfilled in its being, between partners who have turned to one another in truth, who express themselves without reserve and are free of the desire for semblance, there is brought into being a memorable common fruitfulness which is to be found nowhere else.

—Martin Buber[13]

Exercise 4.4. Group Dialogue

Communication is a central feature in Senge's model of organizational learning.[14] In his model, one of his learning disciplines is dialogue, or *team learning.* At this point, the team members will apply many of their skills learned throughout the workshop in a group dialogue session.

Dialogue is a form of conversation characterized by openness and candor, mutual inquiry and learning, authenticity, and mutual confirmation. See chapter 6 for many good resources for learning about dialogue.[15] Adapted from W. Isaacs, the guidelines for this dialogue session appear in overhead 4.29.[16]

 Facilitator: Show and read overhead 4.29.

Explain the guidelines:

- *Suspend assumptions and certainties.* Each of us has many assumptions, opinions, positions, and beliefs. In dialogue, we need to suspend them for a while so that we can make inquiries with an open mind. Suspending our assumptions and certainties opens up the way to learning with other people, particularly people who are different from us.

> *Guidelines for Dialogue*
>
> - Suspend assumptions and certainties.
> - Observe the observer.
> - Listen to your listening.
> - Slow down the inquiry.
> - Befriend polarization.
>
> **4.29** Adapted from W. Isaacs, "Taking Flight: Dialogue, Collective Thinking, and Organizational Learning," *Organizational Dynamics* 22, no. 2 (1993).   © 2001 Joshua D. Geller

- *Observe the observer.* Watch yourself and your reactions. What are you thinking? What are you seeing? Why do you perceive and process information in this way? In an unstructured dialogue, we can learn from reflecting on what we think, do, and say.

- *Listen to your listening.* How well are you listening? Do your assumptions affect your perception? Are you listening below the surface to the feelings, commitments, and implications behind what is said?

- *Slow down the inquiry.* There is no hurry. Even silence is good. No decisions have to be made and no problems solved. Dialogue has no clear end or beginning. The inquiry remains open.

- *Befriend polarization.* Conflict is just a stage in the unfolding of a dialogue. People are different, and the thinking behind what people do or do not do and say or do not say is different. Dialogue opens up these differences. When you discover difference, befriend it. Difference is a source of learning, synergy, and creativity when you work your way through it.

The dialogue in this exercise is fairly unstructured. Allow as much time as you reasonably can, anywhere from ten minutes to half an hour. Varying the length of the dialogue gives you an opportunity to adjust for the time available and the pace of the group. Select a good, open-ended topic for the group, and ask the participants to focus their dialogue on the topic. Some good topics are:

- Communication in the organization where they work
- Communication at work (if the participants are from different organizations)
- Human relationships at work
- Leadership and communication

To facilitate the dialogue, simply state the guidelines and the topic. Ask if anyone has any questions, and then let them talk. Intervene if any members do not follow the guidelines. Near the end you can ask questions, such as:

- How well did we follow the guidelines for dialogue?
- Who were you in the conversation today?
- What is your evaluation of dialogue as a method for learning?

After debriefing the dialogue, transition to the final segment by quickly reviewing the five conversations. This last conversation—learning and completion—leads to the final topic of development planning.

Personal Development Plan

Time for segment: 40 minutes

Here the participants create their own development plans. This activity builds on the participants' development plans from the end of the other three workshop modules.

PERSONAL DEVELOPMENT PLAN

Step 1. Reflection

Revisit the commitments you worked on earlier. Take some time to read and reflect on workbook activities 4.1 through 4.3, which outline your current, future, and prioritized commitments.

Step 2. Mission

Write your professional mission statement, declaring what you want to accomplish in your work. Usually a mission statement is brief. Examples of personal mission statements are:

- To innovate new uses for information technology that improve the effectiveness of people and organizations
- To help people develop in their work
- To help people through improving administrative processes in hospitals
- To create unique visual art characteristic of women's experience

My professional mission statement is:

_____

_____

_____

_____

_____

_____

_____

_____

_____

_____

Step 3. Creative Tension

Write two brief essays. In the first essay, assess your current reality. Take a good look and answer the following questions: What is the reality of your behavior? Your connections and networks? Your performance? Are other members of your organization eager to have you as part of their team?

My current reality:

_____

_____

_____

_____

_____

_____

_____

_____

_____

_____

_____

_____

_____

_____

_____

_____

_____

_____

_____

Step 3. Creative Tension (Continued)

Now write a brief essay about the ideal future. Consider these questions: What kind of work relationships would you like to have? What results do you want? What connections and networks do you want? What communication skills would you like to master?

My ideal future:

_____

_____

_____

_____

_____

_____

_____

_____

_____

_____

_____

_____

_____

_____

_____

_____

_____

_____

_____

_____

_____

_____

Step 4. Potential Areas for Development

Next select an area for development. Consider the following criteria.

- The development goal would be a *breakthrough* for you in your relationships with others.
- The goal is *concrete*—that is, you and others can observe whether you perform the behavior.
- The *results* of the goal are observable. For example, if you perform the behavior well, you will observe its positive effects in others and in your relationships.
- You select the goal freely and feel an *internal commitment* toward this goal.

In the space below, write your goal.

Brainstorm potential areas for development:

Step 5. Development Plan 1

Your commitment to development (identify concrete behaviors):

_____

_____

_____

_____

Why you have selected this goal:

_____

_____

_____

_____

How you will accomplish this goal (include research, plans, behaviors):

_____

_____

_____

_____

Others who can help you accomplish this goal:

_____

_____

_____

How you will follow up and know if you are successful:

_____

_____

_____

_____

Development Plan 2

Your commitment to development (identify concrete behaviors):

_____

_____

_____

_____

Why you have selected this goal:

_____

_____

_____

_____

How you will accomplish this goal (include research, plans, behaviors):

_____

_____

_____

_____

Others who can help you accomplish this goal:

_____

_____

_____

How you will follow up and know if you are successful:

_____

_____

_____

_____

Development Plan 3

Your commitment to development (identify concrete behaviors):

_____

_____

_____

_____

Why you have selected this goal:

_____

_____

_____

_____

How you will accomplish this goal (include research, plans, behaviors):

_____

_____

_____

_____

Others who can help you accomplish this goal:

_____

_____

_____

How you will follow up and know if you are successful:

_____

_____

_____

_____

Step 1. Reflection
The participants first revisit the commitments they worked on earlier. Ask them to read and reflect on workbook activities 4-1 through 4-3—their current, future, and prioritized commitments.

Step 2. Mission
In step 2 of the development plan, the participants write their professional *mission statements,* or declarations of what they want to do and accomplish in their work. Usually a mission statement is brief. Examples of personal mission statements are:

- To innovate new uses for information technology that improve the effectiveness of people and organizations
- To help people develop in their work
- To help people through improving administrative processes in hospitals
- To create unique visual art characteristic of women's experience

Ask them to make their mission statements clear, compelling, and brief—one sentence is best. Instruct the participants to write and rewrite their mission statements in their workbooks. Circulate and help.

Step 3. Creative Tension
> *Creative tension* is the difference we feel between current reality and the way we would like things to be.[17] In this step, you write two short essays. The first essay describes your current state. Take a good look at reality. What is the reality of your behavior? What is the reality of your connections and networks? What is the reality of your performance? Ask yourself the question, Are other members of your organization eager to have you as part of the team?
> In the second essay describe the way you would like things to be. This statement is your vision of the future.

Give the participants five minutes to write each essay. Let them know when the first five minutes are up, and instruct them to move to the second essay.

Step 4. Brainstorm Potential Development Areas
Given all of the insights the participants have gathered throughout the workshop, it is time to identify those that are most actionable. Development in communication works. There are many stories about how people overcame a lack of skill and became extraordinary communicators. Mohandas Gandhi, for example, lacked skill and confidence when he first started speaking in public. Over time, Gandhi became a great, world-renowned communicator. Examples of business people who overcame obstacles to become good communicators are Jack Welch, CEO of General Electric, and Bob Davis, CEO of Lycos. Instruct the participants to brainstorm first and then rank potential development areas on the worksheet.

Step 5. Development Plan

At the end of each session, the participants identified areas for development. Now they should synthesize them.

> What one or two development areas would be a breakthrough for you? What one or two development areas would enable you to accomplish your mission and commitments? The more focus the better. Do not work on more than three areas.

Give the participants ten minutes to complete one or more plans in the workbook. Circulate and help the participants as they write their plans.

Exercise 4.5. Presenting a Goal to the Group

Inform the participants they are each invited to make an informal presentation to the whole group. Their presentations should have two parts. In the first part state what key insight or learning they had during the workshop, and in the second part they present one of their development plans. Ask the participants to describe one of their goals, the related behaviors and skills, their plan for development, and how they will follow up and determine whether they are successful.

Ask the participants to practice a declarative speech act. Remind them of the powerful speech forms practiced in module 2 on assertiveness. Avoid the "ums" and "ahs," disclaimers, hedges, and tentative words such as "try" or "might." Suggest they begin with the phrase "I will." After each person speaks, the class can express their appreciation with applause.

WORKSHOP CONCLUSION

You want to consider your closing carefully. Everyone in the room has invested considerable energy in the workshop, and now you need to provide closure and appreciation. The ending needs to be powerful, because it communicates the session's value. The following material is one example. Customize it to fit your needs.

> During our time together we have taken the opportunity to develop our own skills, and looking around the room I see some breakthroughs. But how do you perpetuate your development when you return to everyday work?
>
> *Transformation* is described as a shift of identity and perspective, or a change in how we think about our lives and ourselves. Transformation is based on communication. A working definition for *transformational learning* includes learning that alters a person's point of view about himself in relationship with others and with the world in which he lives and works to become more authentic, empathic, and functionally effective.

For me transformation is a lifelong event that evolves during the seasons of life—the springtime when we are young, and summer, autumn, and winter. Vincent Van Gogh once said, "Great things are not done by impulse, but by a series of small things brought together." Transformation is akin to a huge project that a lifetime might not be long enough to fulfill.

So, the first feature, which strikes me as being true about working on both personal and organizational transformation, represents a positive, hopeful orientation toward the future. I like to remember the words of the great Roman sage Marcus Aurelius Antoninus:

If you are distressed by anything external,
The pain is not due to the thing itself
But to your estimate of it;
And this you have the power to revoke at any moment.

We have the power to see our lives, relationships, and organizations positively. Remember self-talk. Cajole the participants into saying together:

- I feel like smiling.

- I am happy.

- I am alive.

An orientation of hope toward the future is, in the words of a poet, "the pull of the future stronger than the pull of the past." It is aspiration that enables change. Personal transformation concerns the meaningfulness of our relationships with others. Although transformation is fueled from within, it reaches its fulfillment in our relationships and in our communities.

In this workshop we covered a great deal of ground. We focused on listening as a communication tool for transformation, for answering the need of others to be heard. We dealt with the problems of perception and discovered how perception is creative. In transformation we gain the skills to coach ourselves and others by perceiving our potentials.

When we take the time to be authentic, we touch upon transformation. To me, authenticity is a great mystery, and the mystery I see working is how authenticity, particularly authenticity with empathy, increases functional effectiveness in everyday life.

We covered many tools for transformation and communication in this workshop. How do we develop these tools? Seminars, courses, and books are helpful, but the best tools are constant observation and practice.

Transformation, when it happens, makes us vulnerable. It opens us to our deepest pain and involves us in forgiveness. We live in a purposeful universe, where suffering makes the heart sincere.

If we look at our world and its suffering, we see a dramatic need for transformation. And in order to aid global change, we must be involved in our own transformation, which involves great optimism and a positive attitude toward ourselves and others.

Consider ending with a story. Appropriate stories are about struggles and breakthroughs. Otherwise, you can challenge the participants to use what they have learned. Remind them: "If you do not use it, you lose it. Use it, and it is yours."

NOTES

1. R. Grudin, *Time and the Art of Living* (New York: Houghton Mifflin, 1997).
2. Grudin, *Time and the Art of Living,* 17.
3. W. Bennis and P. Biederman, *Organizing Genius: The Secrets of Creative Collaboration* (Reading, MA: Addison-Wesley, 1998).
4. D. Goleman, *Emotional Intelligence* (New York: Bantam, 1997), and H. Weisinger, *Emotional Intelligence at Work,* 2d ed. (San Francisco: Jossey-Bass, 2000).
5. Roger von Oech, *A Whack on the Side of the Head: How You Can Be More Creative,* rev. ed. (New York: Warner Books, 1998).
6. N. Postman, *The End of Education: Redefining the Value of School* (New York: Vintage Books 1996).
7. For an explanation of networks, see K. Miller's *Oganizational Communication: Approaches and Processes* (Belmont, CA: Wadsworth, 1999).
8. R. M. Kanter, *The Change Masters: Innovation and Entrepreneurship in the American Corporation* (New York: Simon & Schuster, 1985), and R. Kaplan, "Trade Routes: The Manager's Network of Relationships," *Organizational Dynamics* (spring 1984): 37–52.
9. A good resource for applied speech act theory is T. Winograd and F. Flores's *Understanding Computers and Cognition: A New Foundation for Design* (Reading, MA: Addison-Wesley, 1986).
10. Oech, *A Whack on the Side of the Head,* 157.
11. See, for example, P. Senge, *The Fifth Discipline: The Art and Practice of the Learning Organization* (New York: Doubleday, 1994), and C. Argyris, *Overcoming Organizational Defenses: Facilitating Organizational Learning* (Needham Heights, MA: Allyn & Bacon, 1990).
12. V. Marsick and K. Watkins, "Organizational Learning," in *What Works: Assessment, Development, and Measurement,* ed. L. Bassie and D. Russ-Eft (Alexandria, VA: American Society for Training and Development, 1997) page 65.
13. M. Buber, *Elements of the Interhuman,* ed. Maurice Friedman, trans. R. Smith, as appears in J. Steward, Ed., *Bridges Not Walls,* 7th ed. (New York: McGraw-Hill 1999), pp. 579–590.
14. P. Senge, *The Fifth Discipline: The Art and Practice of the Learning Organization* (New York: Doubleday, 1994).
15. See, for example, D. Bohm, *On Dialogue,* ed. L. Nichol (New York: Routledge, 1996); M. Buber, *The Knowledge of Man,* ed. M. Freedman and trans. R. G. Smith, Humanity Books, 1988; W. Isaacs, "Taking Flight: Dialogue, Collective Thinking, and Organizational Learning," *Organizational*

Dynamics 22, no. 2 (1993): 24–39; and W. Isaacs, *Dialogue and the Art of Thinking Together* (New York: Doubleday, 1999).

16. The guidelines are adapted from Isaacs, "Taking Flight."

17. Senge, *The Fifth Discipline;* P. Senge, C. Roberts, R. B. Ross, B. J. Smith, and A. Kleiner, *The Fifth Discipline Fieldbook* (New York: Currency Doubleday, 1994), and N. Tichy and N. Cohen, *The Leadership Engine: How Winning Companies Build Leaders at Every Level* (New York: Harper Business, 1997).

PART III

EVALUATION AND FOLLOW-UP

Evaluation and Follow-Up

Yvonne stands before the top management team to present her quarterly review of the training function. At the team's request, Yvonne had implemented the *Interpersonal Communication Workshop*, making it available to all departments. Because more than half the employees—or 200 people—participated, this effort represents a large investment. Now the CEO asks Yvonne, "How do you know this workshop has contributed to our bottom line?"

Yvonne is prepared. Would you be?

According to R. S. Caffarella, *program evaluation* is "a process used to determine whether the design and delivery of a program were effective and whether the proposed outcomes were met."[1] *Formative evaluation* occurs while the training is in process, and *summative evaluation* occurs after the training is complete.

With the Interpersonal Communication Workshop, the purposes of evaluation are to:

- Give data for improving the program.
- Focus the trainer on participant learning.
- Encourage a training design with clear objectives for the participants.
- Help the transfer of learning.
- Provide accountability for the workshop.
- Demonstrate the achievements of the program.

Measuring educational effectiveness often poses a dilemma for trainers. On the one hand, without measuring their effectiveness, trainers have no good way to improve their programs. Also, a lack of thorough measurement could be embarrassing for the training function. On the other hand, thorough measurement can be time consuming, difficult, and invasive. The predicament of whether to conduct an evaluation can be like hovering above a bull's two horns—neither alternative seems attractive.

This unit gives recommended options for evaluating the Interpersonal Communication Workshop. Measuring the effectiveness of training programs must be integrated with other facets of instruction, such as:

- Existing measures—for example, needs assessments
- Instructional objectives
- Corporate cultures and norms
- Trainees' availability and participation
- Budgets and resources (measurement can be expensive)
- Reporting and review processes for the training function
- Client preferences
- Objectives of measurement—for example, program improvement, instructor development, and demonstration of program accomplishments

Given your measurement objectives, design your data collection, analysis, and reporting appropriately.

Collect participant feedback using the Participant Feedback questionnaire shown in figure 5.1. Questions address variables such as the session objectives, instructor competence, and relevance of material. The questionnaire also asks participants for open-ended feedback. Questionnaire results give evidence of the effectiveness of training. Use the results to identify strengths and weaknesses and to improve the workshop through time.

Conduct your formative evaluation during instruction. The lecture notes describe the knowledge and skills highlighted in each session. In formative evaluation, you determine how well the participants demonstrate this knowledge and skill. After each session enter notes on the instructor's self-evaluation sheet (see figure 5.2).

The workshop has many activities in which the participants interact with each other using a particular conversational design. When the participants practice using I statements with each other, for example, you can observe their performance and assess their competence. Also, you can evaluate their motivation to use these statements by monitoring their comments in the debrief that follows each activity. The major contribution of formative evaluation is to improve your instruction, which you can expedite during the workshop by adapting to the participants' responses.

Not everyone will master all of the content. Often they will select the competencies that are most relevant for them. Figure 5.2 is a template for evaluating the learning during specific activities. In the first section, describe how well participants learned the material. Refer to specific knowledge, skills, and motivations. In the second section describe what you want to improve. You can photocopy this sheet and use as many copies as you like.

FIGURE 5.1

PARTICIPANT FEEDBACK

Your feedback on the workshop will help to improve it. Please answer the questions below.

Date: _____

Please circle the number that best represents your reaction to the workshop.

1 = Disagree 2 = Somewhat disagree 3 = Neutral 4 = Somewhat agree 5 = Agree

1. The objectives of the workshop were clear.   1   2   3   4   5
   If less than 3, please explain: _____
   _____
   _____

2. The instructor's delivery met professional expectations.1   2   3   4   5
   If less than 3, please explain: _____
   _____
   _____

3. The instructor knew the material well.   1   2   3   4   5
   If less than 3, please explain: _____
   _____
   _____

4. The instructor helped you learn.   1   2   3   4   5
   If less than 3, please explain: _____
   _____
   _____

5. The techniques and activities helped you learn.   1   2   3   4   5
   If less than 3, please explain: _____
   _____
   _____

6. The materials presented met your needs.   1   2   3   4   5
   If less than 3, please explain: _____
   _____
   _____

(continued)

7. You will be able to apply these skills to your work.   1 2 3 4 5

   If less than 3, please explain: _____

   _____

   _____

8. Overall, you would rate the workshop as excellent.   1 2 3 4 5

   If less than 3, please explain: _____

   _____

   _____

9. What were the major strengths of the program?

   _____

   _____

   _____

   _____

   _____

10. What about the program could be improved?

   _____

   _____

   _____

   _____

   _____

11. What workshop material will you use on the job? What workshop
    material will not be used on the job?

   _____

   _____

   _____

   _____

   _____

   _____

12. What else would you like to say about this workshop?

   _____

   _____

   _____

   _____

   _____

   _____

Thank you for your response.

FIGURE 5.2

INSTRUCTOR'S SELF-EVALUATION SHEET

Page ___ of ___

Date: _____   Workshop Module: _____

Use this form to describe how well participants learned specific workshop content and to identify ways you can improve instruction.

Topic/Competency _____

How well participants learned the material:

_____
_____
_____
_____

What could be improved?

_____
_____
_____
_____

Topic/Competency _____

How well participants learned the material:

_____
_____
_____
_____

What could be improved?

_____
_____
_____
_____

Agreements and Notes:

_____
_____
_____
_____
_____
_____
_____
_____

Below is an example of notes from a formative evaluation. You will have to write your notes from memory following your sessions, because, as the instructor, you won't have time to record more than a brief reference during the sessions.

This example is from module 3's conflict game of peril. In this game, the participants demonstrate their knowledge of the content covered throughout the session.

How well participants learned the material:
There was a variance in how well participants learned this material. Out of twenty trainees, only two-thirds were ready to answer most of the questions. No one answered satisfactorily the question in the conflict styles and archetypes section (40 points): What is the difference between compromise and collaboration? Four participants did not offer any responses during the game.

What can be improved?
The game worked well as a test and a review. They enjoyed the game, and I believe the participants benefited from the review. I have to use better examples and check for understanding when I teach the difference between compromise and collaboration. I need to engage the quiet people more so I can determine if they learned the material.

FOLLOW-UP FEEDBACK ON BEHAVIOR

Workshops can become a blur from the past once people return to work. Also, the major breakdown in the training process is the transfer of learning to the workplace. Module 4, "Communicating for Action," concludes with a personal development plan for the participants that serves as the first step in evaluating changes in behavior.

The steps in using follow-up feedback on behavior appear below.

1. Have participants complete the development plans during the workshop. You can use this plan for the whole workshop or for individual modules.

2. Make sure all participants have a coach in the organization and that they inform their coaches about their development plans.

3. Instruct the participants to use a development journal. In the journal, they will record any critical incidents regarding their development area. Also, they will evaluate their progress regularly—once a week, for example.

4. The coaches and participants schedule half-hour follow-up meetings once a week for a month. They will use the workshop follow-up sheet to record all progress (see figure 5.3).

5. Assemble a focus group of randomly selected participants and coaches to talk about their progress on the development plans. Collect data during this meeting. Also, collect copies of their workshop follow-up sheets and analyze them.

FIGURE 5.3

WORKSHOP FOLLOW-UP SHEET

Page ___ of ___

Date: _____   Name: _____

This form serves to organize conversations between you and your mentor regarding your ongoing development following the Interpersonal Communication Workshop.

Development area _____

Behaviors you want to change or learn:

_____
_____
_____
_____

Situation:

_____
_____
_____
_____

Your plan to apply these skills:

_____
_____
_____
_____

Progress and critical incidents:

_____
_____
_____
_____

Notes:

_____
_____
_____
_____
_____
_____
_____
_____
_____

ANECDOTAL EVIDENCE

Quantitative data are difficult to collect regarding training in interpersonal communication. Often the cost is not worth it. Anecdotal evidence of performance improvement, on the other hand, can be easier to collect and quite compelling.

Anecdotal evidence is primarily qualitative because it is based on collected stories about the training's effects. The main criticism of anecdotal evidence is the researcher might be biased, particularly if this researcher is the instructor—that is, someone who has an interest in the program's success and image. Therefore, be as rigorous in gathering your evidence as possible. Try to involve others who are objective and trained in qualitative methods to collect these data. Also, remember the limitations of this kind of research: It is subjective, it is evidence rather than proof, and it reveals a rich description about the experience of particular people or groups.

To collect anecdotal evidence, follow these steps:

1. Select people, teams, or organizations that represent those who have participated in the training.

2. Ask for an interview with these people or representatives of larger units.

3. Prepare your questions for the interview. Here are some ideas:

- What was your evaluation of the training session?

- What, if anything, would you change about the training?

- What connections do you see between the competencies learned in the training and your performance (or the performance of your team)?

- Tell me a story or about critical incidents that demonstrate the effectiveness of your training.

- Share any numbers or data related to changes in your performance.

- What else might have affected these numbers?

- What advice do you have about how to improve this training?

- What else would you like to say regarding the workshop?

4. Ask also if you may quote the respondents or if they want their responses to remain confidential. The next step is to analyze the data and write the report.

COMPLETION

Evaluating and reporting your results give you a chance to complete at least a cycle of your work. Whereas evaluation and reporting lead to program revision and improvement, they also give you a chance to stop and reflect on your performance. Further, this process provides a chance to celebrate, share, and acknowledge the accomplishments of those involved. Do not lose this opportunity to recognize them.

The first task is to reflect on your own work. As soon as possible following the workshop, review and summarize your evaluation data.

Use the same techniques outlined in module 4 for your own personal development plan. Workbook activity 4.5 provides a process with five steps:

- Revisit your mission—what did you want to accomplish?
- Describe current reality—assess your performance and your results.
- Describe how you would like the workshop to go next time.
- Identify concrete areas for your personal development.
- Plan, implement, and monitor your development.

Also, take time to celebrate yourself. Focus on your strengths, and appreciate your accomplishments. Even your mistakes are grist for the mill, or something you can learn from. Next, do the same exercise with your partners.

Too few teams debrief their work and learn from their experiences as a group. Make the evaluation process a chance to reconnect with your partners in the workshop. Meet and have a conversation in which you:

- Identify and celebrate what went well.
- Express your appreciation for the contribution of particular people and groups.
- Identify what can be shared about learning or what you would do differently next time.
- Plan to follow up and decide what you will share with other groups that would be interested in and could benefit from what you learned.

Evaluation time is an opportunity to communicate the value of the program, especially with the levels of management that sponsored the program.

How did Yvonne prepare for the CEO's question regarding whether the Interpersonal Communication Skills Workshop contributed to the organization's bottom line? Yvonne followed this chapter's recommendations and evaluated her program.

First, Yvonne compiled the results of both the participant feedback survey, which show that the participants had a positive regard for the sessions and the instructor, and the focus groups that followed up on the changes in the participants' behaviors. Finally, Yvonne gathered strong anecdotal evidence from several important groups within the company about how the training had helped them improve their relationships and performance. One of the vice-presidents present at the CEO's meeting led one of these groups, and his strong testimony at the review helped solidify everything Yvonne had to say.

Like Yvonne, through careful evaluation of your workshop you can improve your instruction and have ready evidence of the workshop's value and success.

NOTE

1. R. S. Caffarella, *Planning Programs for Adult Learners* (San Francisco: Jossey-Bass, 1994), 119.

RESOURCES for TRAINERS

Today, training has grown into one of the most critical success requirements in a highly competitive global marketplace.

— Tom Goad (1997)

This chapter provides resources for instructor development. Trainers should consult the following books, articles, and professional organizations when preparing to teach The Interpersonal Communication Skills Workshop.

Some of the following resources are cited throughout this book. The other resources provide a broad and deep background in communication practice and theory related to the workshop. The section begins with general resources and then lists resources specific to each chapter.

GENERAL RESOURCES

Books

Mitchell, G. *The Trainer's Handbook.* 3d ed. New York: AMACOM, 1998.

Rothwell, W. J., and H. J. Sredl. *The ASTD Reference Guide to Professional Human Resource Development Roles and Competencies.* 2d ed. Amherst, MA: HRD Press, 1992.

Stolovitch, H. D., and E. J. Keeps. *Handbook of Human Performance Technology: Improving Individual and Organizational Performance Worldwide.* 2d ed. San Francisco: Jossey-Bass, 1999.

Associations

AMACOM (online): http://www.amacombooks.org

AMACOM publishes books for the American Management Association on various management topics including training and development.

The American Management Association (online): http://www.amanet.org

The American Management Association is the leading organization in the field of management development. For more information on AMA call 1-800-262-9699.

American Society for Training and Development (online): http://www.astd.org

International Association of Business Communicators (online): http://www.iabc.com/homepage.htm

The International Communication Association (online): http://www.icahdq.org

The International Communication Association specializes in research and dialogue about communication interests.

National Communication Association (online): http://www.natcom.org

The National Communication Association deals with the study, criticism, research, teaching, and application of scientific and humanistic principles of communication. For more information on NCA, call 1-847-491-7023.

RESOURCES FOR INTRODUCTION

Books

Caffarella, R. S. *Planning Programs for Adult Learners.* San Francisco: Jossey-Bass, 1994.

This good book explains the details of planning adult education programs. It includes a planning model on the following topics: integrating partners, setting goals and objectives, project management, instruction, budgeting, marketing, setting up facilities, and evaluation.

Carr, C. *Smart Training.* New York: McGraw-Hill, 1992.

Carr's great book addresses the transfer of learning.

Goad, T.W. *The First-Time Trainer.* New York: AMACOM, 1997.

Morreale, S. P., B. H. Spitzberg, and J. K. Barge. *Human Communication: Motivation, Knowledge, and Skills.* Belmont, CA: Wadsworth, 2000.

Rothwell, W. J., and H. C. Kazanas. *Mastering the Instructional Design Process: A Systematic Approach.* 2d ed. San Francisco: Jossey-Bass, 1998.

Rothwell, W., J. Sullivan, A. Roland, and G. N. McLean. *Practicing Organizational Development: A Guide for Consultants.* San Francisco: Pfeiffer, 1995.

RESOURCES FOR MODULE 1. POWERFUL LISTENING

Books

Adler, R. B., L. B. Rosenfeld, and N. Towne. *Interplay: The Process of Interpersonal Communication.* 7th ed. New York: Harcourt Brace, 1998.

This book has an excellent chapter on listening. The book describes the research basis for overhead 1.8.

Bone, D., and M. Crisp, eds. *The Business of Listening: A Practical Guide to Effective Listening.* Rev. ed. Menlo Park, CA: Crisp Publications, 1995.

The book provides a good, fast course on listening for business people.

Borisoff, D., and M. Purdy. *Listening in Everyday Life: A Personal and Professional Approach.* 2d ed. New York: University Press in America, 1996.

An excellent, research-based compilation of articles on listening, the book includes a history of research and training in listening as well as excellent chapters on such issues as gender differences in listening.

Burley-Allen, M. *Listening: The Forgotten Skill.* 2d ed. New York: John Wiley and Sons, Inc., 1995.

This guide will teach you how to acquire active, productive listening skills.

Collins, R., and P. J. Cooper. *The Power of Story: Teaching through Storytelling.* 2d ed. New York: Prentice Hall, 1996.

Duggar, J. *Listen Up: Hear What's Really Being Said.* Urbandale, IA: American Media Publishing, 1995.

This book identifies barriers that can impede effective communication processes.

Genua, R. B. *Managing Your Mouth: An Owner's Manual for Your Most Important Asset.* New York: AMACOM, 1993.

This book on listening explains the use of verbal and nonverbal cues in communication. It includes an in-depth assessment and covers such scenarios as controversy, bad news, networking, and gossip.

Lorayne, H. *Page-a-Minute Memory Book.* New York: Ballantine, 1996.

The *Page-a-Minute Memory Book* is an easy-to-use book on improving memory.

Nichols, M. *The Lost Art of Listening.* The Guilford Family Therapy Series. New York: Guilford Press, 1995.

This great book details the psychological aspects of listening, particularly defensiveness and the need to be heard.

Peters, T. J. *In Search of Excellence: Lessons from America's Best-Run Companies.* New York: Warner Books, 1988.

———. *Thriving on Chaos: Handbook for a Management Revolution.* New York: HarperCollins, 1991.

Peters's book devotes three entire sections to listening.

Senge, P., C. Roberts, R. B. Ross, B. J. Smith, and A. Kleiner. *The Fifth Discipline Fieldbook.* New York: Currency Doubleday, 1994.

This great book has many training exercises related to listening.

Slan, J. *Using Stories and Humor: Grab Your Audience.* Needham Heights, MA: Allyn & Bacon, 1998.

Wolvin, A., and C. G. Coakley. *Listening.* 3d ed. Guilford, CT: Brown & Benchmark, 1995.

This book summarizes an important and enormous range of research on listening.

Wood, J. T. *Interpersonal Communication: Everyday Encounters.* Belmont, CA: Wadsworth, 1998.

As well as being a great textbook on interpersonal communication, its chapter 6 on mindful listening is a fine resource for material on listening.

Zuker, E. *The Seven Secrets of Influence.* New York: McGraw-Hill, 1991.

This book identifies six basic influence styles: the telling/analyst, compelling/pragmatist, feeling/preservationist, welling/catalyst, selling/strategist, and gelling/idealist. It also includes exercises to identify personal styles and describes how the use of listening is an influencing skill.

Journal Articles

Barker, L., C. Edwards, K. G. Gaines, and F. Holley. "An Investigation of Proportional Time Spent in Various Communication Activities by College Students." *Journal of Applied Communication Research* 8 (1981): 101–9.

The article provides the research basis for overhead 1.8.

Blodgett, P. C. "Six Ways to Be a Better Listener." *Training and Development* 51, no. 7 (1997): 11–12.

This article discusses and details several ways to improve listening effectiveness.

Clark, K. F. "Say It Again, Sam." *Human Resource Executive* 11, no. 17 (1997): 54–57.

This article examines what is meant by good listening skills and explains how they are becoming more important as businesses cope with such complex problems as global expansion and employee retention.

Harris, R. M. "Turn Listening into a Powerful Presence." *Training and Development* 51, no. 7 (1997): 9–11.

This article summarizes seven ways to improve communication and listening patterns and provides a training learning tool.

Morris, L. "How Effective Are We as Listeners?" *Training and Development* 47, no. 4 (1993): 79–80.

This article reports the results of a survey of managers and their perceived listening skills. It identifies four listening types: active listener, involved listener, passive listener, and detached listener.

Salopek, J. J. "Is Anyone Listening?" *Training and Development* 53, no. 9 (1999): 58–59.

This article explains why listening skills are important, lists ways to become a better listener, and includes a short self-assessment of listening skills.

Audiocassette Tape

Cairo, J. *The Power of Effective Listening* (811). Carol Stream, IL: Oasis Audio, 1999.

This four-cassette learning system teaches the art of active listening and how to hear what is really being said, which, in turn, will help build positive and productive relationships.

Association

International Listening Association (online): http://www.listen.org

The International Listening Association promotes the study, development, and teaching of listening and the practice of effective listening skills and techniques. For more information on the ILA, call 1-800-ILA-4505 or 715-425-3377.

RESOURCES FOR MODULE 2. ASSERTIVENESS
Books

Alberti, R. E., and M. L. Emmons. *Your Perfect Right: A Guide to Assertive Living.* San Luis Obispo, CA: Impact Publishers, Inc., 1995.
The original work on assertiveness training is still an excellent primer.
Bateson, G. *Steps to an Ecology of Mind.* Chicago: University of Chicago Press, 2000.
Bateson's insights as an anthropologist cross over to psychology and interpersonal communication. His work is a basis for the principles of communication and relationships in this module.
Bower, S. A., and G. H. Bower. *Asserting Yourself.* 2d ed. New York: Perseus Books, 1991.
This book will assist you with building an individual assertiveness program by providing exercises to improve your self-esteem, to look and feel assertive, and to develop meaningful friendships.
Canfield, J., and M. V. Hansen. *The Aladdin Factor.* New York: Berkley, 1995.
This book is an excellent read about attitudes, self-worth, and asking for what you deserve.
Davidson, J. *The Complete Idiot's Guide to Assertiveness.* New York: Macmillan, 1997.
Davidson provides a good resource for assertiveness in everyday life.
DeVito, J. A. *The Interpersonal Communication Book.* 8th ed. Reading, MA: Addison-Wesley, 1997.
This book gives a simple overview of interpersonal communication as well as a good synopsis of its underlying principles. Chapter 5 contains a good passage on assertiveness.
Dubrin, A. J. *Your Own Worst Enemy: How to Overcome Career Self-Sabotage.* New York: AMACOM, 1993.
This book shows you how self-destructive mechanisms work and provides concrete advice for breaking the negative pattern. It includes a questionnaire to assist you in identifying your own destructive behaviors and offers suggestions on how to change.
Eiffert, S. D. *Cross-Train Your Brain.* New York: AMACOM, 1999.
This book supplies tools, exercises, and techniques to increase mental effectiveness and creative thinking skills. The book is a great resource for enhancing mental images.
Helmstetter, S. *What to Say When You Talk to Yourself.* New York: Fine Communications, 1997.
This book is about relying on yourself to optimize your outlook, focus your goals, and adapt to the technique of positive self-talk.
Lloyd, S. R. *Developing Positive Assertiveness.* 2d ed. Menlo Park, CA: Crisp Publications, Inc., 1995.
This book explains what assertive behavior is and why it is desirable and important to develop and use.
Lusk, J. T. *30 Scripts for Relaxation, Imagery and Inner Healing,* vol. 2. Duluth, MN: Whole Person Associates Incorporated, 1992.

McKay, M., and P. Fanning. *Self-Esteem: A Proven Program of Cognitive Techniques for Assessing, Improving, and Maintaining Your Self-Esteem.* 3d ed. Oakland, CA: New Harbinger Publications, 2000.

This book outlines step-by-step processes on how to take charge of your self-critical voice, to use visualization for self-acceptance, to handle mistakes and responses to criticism, and to ask for what you really want.

Newman, J. *Wisdom for Earthlings: How to Make Better Choices and Take Action in Your Work.* New York: AMACOM, 1996.

This book is about becoming assertive, effective, healthier, and happier in your job, family, and personal life.

Watzlawick, P., J. H. Beavin, and D. D. Jackson. *Pragmatics of Human Communication: A Study of Interactional Patterns, Pathologies, and Paradoxes.* New York: W. W. Norton, 1967.

This book provided an early foundation for the principles of communication as taught in module 2.

Journal Articles

Er, M. C. "Assertive Behavior and Stress." *Advanced Management Journal* 54, no. 4 (1989): 4–8.

This article describes five different types of assertive behavior. It also explains how the inappropriate use of assertive behavior can lead to stressful work situations.

Harper, S. C. "Business Education: A View from the Top." *Business Forum* 12 (summer 1987): 24–27.

Two hundred deans of business schools and 200 CEOs of corporations identify communication competence as the most important characteristic of top performers.

Morreale, S. P., P. Sherwyn, M. M. Osborn, and J. C. Pearson. "Why Communication Is Important: An Argument Supporting the Centrality of the Communication Discipline." *Journal of the Association of Communication Administrators,* November 1999.

This single article summarizes almost 100 research articles demonstrating the centrality of communication competence to academic, career, and personal success.

Smith-Jentsch, K. A., E. Salas, and D. P. Baker. "Training Team Performance, Related Assertiveness." *Personnel Psychology* 49, no. 4 (1996): 909–936.

This article addresses findings from three studies that examined the determinants of assertiveness in terms of team member interaction.

Audiocassette Tape

Canfield, J. *How to Build High Self-Esteem: A Practical Process for Your Personal Growth* (728A). Niles, IL: Nightingale-Conant Corp, 1989.

This six-cassette learning system will teach you about creating a positive focus; balancing mind, body, and spirit; the power of completion; celebrating your strengths; setting and achieving goals; affirmation; and the power of positive action.

RESOURCES FOR MODULE 3. CONFLICT MANAGEMENT
Books

Bassi, L. J., and D. Russ-Eft. *What Works: Training and Development Practices.* Alexandria, VA: American Society for Training and Development, 1997.

This book has a collection of articles from human resources development experts in five areas: leadership development, conflict management, diversity training, learning technologies, and behavior modeling/modifications. Each article provides implications for practitioners in the field.

Borisoff, D., and D. A. Victor. *Conflict Management: A Communication Skills Approach.* Needham Heights, MA: Allyn & Bacon, 1997.

This book examines the nature of conflict in both oral and written communication. It includes a chapter titled "Cross Cultural Awareness in Conflict Management."

Buber, M. "Elements of the Interhuman," ed. Maurice Friedman, trans. R. Smith, in John Steward's *Bridges Not Walls,* 7th ed. (New York: McGraw-Hill, pp. 579–590.

Capman, E. N., and S. L. O'Neil. *Your Attitude Is Showing: A Primer of Human Relations.* New York: Prentice Hall, 1998.

This book presents human-relations competencies for developing human relationships and dealing with conflict. The book includes twenty-two case studies.

Fisher, R., W. Ury, and B. Patton. *Getting to Yes.* 2d ed. New York: Penguin Books, 1991.

Grant, W. *Resolving Conflicts: How to Turn Conflict into Cooperation.* Boston, MA: Element Books, Inc., 1997.

This book provides practical suggestions for letting go of anger, gives examples of how relationships can grow and change, provides exercises in confidence building, and teaches how to recognize defensive behavior and set positive thinking patterns.

Levine, S. *Getting to Resolution: Turning Conflict into Collaboration.* San Francisco: Berrett-Koehler, 1998.

This book sets out to change patterns about conflict and provides guidelines for creating collaborative agreements. It includes a case study model for resolution.

Lewicki, R. J., D. M. Saunders, and J. W. Minton. *Negotiation.* 3d ed. Boston: McGraw-Hill, 1998.

An excellent compendium, it explains negotiation and conflict management for skilled practitioners.

Lulofs, R., and D. Cahn. *Conflict: From Theory to Action.* Needham Heights, MA: Allyn & Bacon, 2000.

Miller, K. *Organizational Communication: Approaches and Processes.* Belmont, CA: Wadsworth, 1999.

This book has an excellent chapter summarizing conflict management.

Paulson, T. L. *They Shoot Managers, Don't They? Managing Yourself and Leading Others in a Changing World.* Berkeley, CA: Ten Speed Press, 1991.

This book discusses how conflict and change work to make managers better leaders. It includes chapters on developing listening skills, using influence properly, building empowered teams, and learning to take risks

Sashkin, M. *Conflict Style Inventory.* Amherst, MA: Human Resource Development Press, 1995.

This book is intended to determine the reader's conflict style by analyzing eleven short case studies. The book defines five conflict styles: avoiding, smoothing, bargaining, forcing, and problem solving.

Ury, W. *Getting Past No: Negotiating Your Way from Confrontation to Cooperation.* New York: Bantam Books, 1993.

This book is a good follow-on from *Getting to Yes,* with excellent materials on preparing for and participating in negotiations.

Vanslyke, E. *Listening to Conflict: Finding Constructive Solutions to Workplace Disputes.* New York: AMACOM, 1999.

Weisinger, H. *The Power of Positive Criticism.* New York: AMACOM, 1999.

This book looks at criticism without negativity and helps to build relationships and increase individual and organizational success.

Journal Article

Bohan, G. P. "Build, Don't Battle." *Training and Development Journal* 44, no. 2 (1990): 15–18.

This article provides tips and suggestions for resolving conflicts in work groups.

Audiocassette Tape

Miller, T. *Self-Discipline and Emotional Control* (10360). Boulder, CO: Career-Track Seminars Publications, 1999.

This six-cassette learning system teaches you how to change your own behaviors and how to determine your emotional and behavioral reactions.

Associations

The Academy of Management, Conflict Management Division (online): http://www.aom.pace.edu/cmd/

The Conflict Management Division of the Academy of Management supports research, teaching, and practice in conflict, power, and negotiation. The Academy of Management is the leading professional association for research and education in the United States.

The Conflict Management Institute (online): http://www.mediate.com/rubenstein/

The Conflict Management Institute is an organization whose mission is to reduce the cost of conflict in the workplace and society, both in monetary and human terms. CMI provides mediation, training, and consultation services that help create workplaces where interpersonal conflict is easily identified, rapidly resolved, and used as an opportunity to enhance teamwork.

Conflict Resolution Center International (online): http://www.conflictres.org

The Conflict Resolution Center International builds conflict resolution principles, knowledge, and techniques; and creates a network for experts to support, analyze, and critique the work of conflict resolvers.

Conflict Resolution Education Network (online): http://www.crenet.org

The Conflict Resolution Education Network is the primary national and international organization for information, resources, and technical assistance in conflict resolution and education.

Society of Professionals in Dispute Resolution (online): http://www.spidr.org/ocm/htm

The Society of Professionals in Dispute Resolution helps members to develop integrated organizational conflict management systems for the purpose of organizational improvement in the area of conflict management. For more information on the SPIDR, call 513-873-1126.

RESOURCES FOR MODULE 4. CONVERSATIONS FOR COORDINATING ACTION

Books

Argyris, C. *Overcoming Organizational Defenses: Facilitating Organizational Learning.* Needham Heights, MA: Allyn & Bacon, 1990.

Argyris, C., and D. A. Schon. *Organizational Learning II: Theory, Method and Practice.* Reading, MA: Addison-Wesley, 1996.

Bateson, G. *Steps to an Ecology of Mind.* Chicago: University of Chicago Press, 2000.

Bennis, W., and P. Biederman. *Organizing Genius: The Secrets of Creative Collaboration.* Reading, MA: Addison-Wesley, 1998.

Block, P. *Flawless Consulting.* 2d ed. San Francisco: Jossey-Bass, 2000.

Bohm, D. *On Dialogue.* Edited by L. Nichol. New York: Routledge, 1996.

Buber, M. *I and Thou.* Translated by R. Smith. New York: Macmillan, 1974.

———. *The Knowledge of Man.* Edited by M. Freedman and translated by R. G. Smith. New York: Humanity Books, 1988.

DeBono, E. *Lateral Thinking: Creativity Step-By-Step.* New York: Harper Collins, 1990.

Goleman, D. *Emotional Intelligence.* New York: Bantam, 1997.

Grudin, R. *Time and the Art of Living.* New York: Houghton Mifflin, 1997.

Hargrove, R. *Masterful Coaching Fieldbook.* San Francisco: Jossey-Bass, 1999.

Isaacs, W. *Dialogue and the Art of Thinking Together.* New York: Doubleday, 1999.

Johnson, C., and M. Hackman. *Creative Communication: Principles and Applications.* Prospect Heights, IL: Waveland Press, 1994.

These authors pull together the scholarly and applied literature related to communication and creativity.

Kanter, R. M. *The Change Masters: Innovation and Entrepreneurship in the American Corporation.* New York: Simon & Schuster, 1985.

Miller, K. *Organizational Communication: Approaches and Processes.* Belmont, CA: Wadsworth, 1999.

This book has an excellent chapter summarizing conflict management.

Oech, Roger von. *A Whack on the Side of the Head: How You Can Be More Creative.* Rev. ed. New York: Warner Books, 1998.

Filled with activities, insights, and stories, this great book for trainers is about creativity.

Senge, P. *The Fifth Discipline: The Art and Practice of the Learning Organization.* New York: Doubleday, 1994.

Tichy, N., and N. Cohen. *The Leadership Engine: How Winning Companies Build Leaders at Every Level.* New York: Harper Business, 1997.

Weisinger, H. *Emotional Intelligence at Work.* 2d ed. San Francisco: Jossey-Bass, 2000.

Winograd, T., and F. Flores. *Understanding Computers and Cognition: A New Foundation for Design.* Reading, MA: Addison-Wesley, 1986.

Journal Articles

Isaacs, W. "Taking Flight: Dialogue, Collective Thinking, and Organizational Learning." *Organizational Dynamics* 22, no. 2 (1993): 24–39.

Kaplan, R. "Trade Routes: The Manager's Network of Relationships." *Organizational Dynamics* (spring 1984): 37–52.

RESOURCES FOR MODULE 5. EVALUATION AND FOLLOW-UP
Books

Bassie, L., and D. Russ-Eft, eds. *What Works: Assessment, Development, and Measurement.* Alexandria, VA: American Society for Training and Development, 1997.

This book includes information on qualitative measurement and organizational learning.

Caffarella, R. S. *Planning Programs for Adult Learners.* San Francisco: Jossey-Bass, 1994.

Callahan, M. "The Role of the Performance Evaluator." *Info-line.* Alexandria, VA: American Society for Training and Development, 1998; issue 9803.

Goad, T. W. *The First-Time Trainer.* New York: AMACOM, 1997.

Kirkpatrick, D. L. *Another Look at Evaluating Training Programs.* Alexandria, VA: American Society for Training and Development, 1998a.

———. *Evaluating Training Programs: The Four Levels.* San Francisco: Berrett-Koehler Publishers, 1998b.

Marsick, V., and K. Watkins. "Organizational Learning." In *What Works: Assessment, Development, and Measurement,* edited by L. Bassie and D. Russ-Eft. Alexandria, VA: American Society for Training and Development, 1997.

Merwin, S. *Evaluation: 10 Significant Ways for Measuring and Improving Training Impact.* San Francisco: Jossey-Bass, 1999.

This straightforward primer is mostly about writing evaluation questions.

Phillips, J. *Handbook of Training Evaluation and Measurement Methods.* 3d ed. Houston, TX: Gulf Publishing, 1997a.

———. *Return on Investment in Training and Performance Improvement.* Houston, TX: Gulf Publishing, 1997b.

APPENDIX A

OVERHEADS

Interpersonal Communication Workshop

Powerful skills for relational intelligence and breakthrough performance

1.1

Workshop Agenda

- Day 1
  - *Morning session: Powerful listening*
  - *Afternoon session: Assertiveness*
- Day 2
  - *Morning session: Conflict management*
  - *Afternoon session: Conversations for coordinating action*

1.2

Workshop Objectives

- Personal and organizational performance

- Effective conflict management

- Interpersonal assertiveness and advocacy

- Powerful listening

1.3

Module Agenda

Total time: Four hours

- Introduction
- Element 1. Volition
- Element 2. Attending
- Element 3. Understanding

1.4

Module Agenda (Cont.)

- Break: Fifteen minutes

- Element 4. Memory

- Element 5. Responding

- Element 6. Development

- Conclusion

1.5

Purpose

To develop the features of powerful listening required to build:

- relationships
- partnerships
- alliances

1.6

The Powerful Listening Model

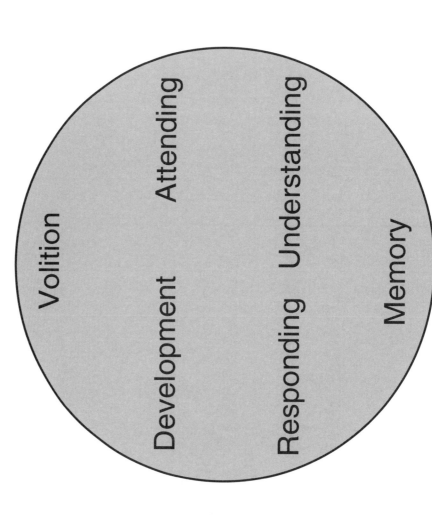

1.7

Time Spent Listening

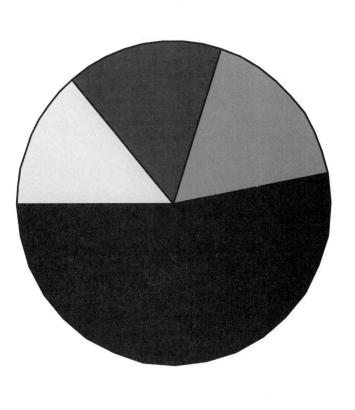

- ☐ Writing, 14%
- ■ Speaking, 16%
- ▨ Reading, 17%
- ■ Listening, 53%

1.8

Chinese Character for Listening

Eyes

The ear

One

The king

Heart

The right side means "virtue."

1.9

Principles for Attending

- Empathy
- Confirmation
- Nonjudgment
- Deep listening

Skills for Active Listening

- Stop, look, and listen.

- Use minimal encouragers—"ah, so?"

- Paraphrase—content and feeling.

- Use minimal inquiry.

Perception Quotes

"Listen to me for a day . . . an hour! . . . a moment! Lest I expire in my lonely silence? O God, is there no one to listen?"

—Seneca

1.12

Perception Quotes (Cont.)

"You and I do not see things as they are. We see things as we are."

—Herb Cohen

1.13

Perception

1.14

Problems of Perception

- Reacting emotionally and defensively.

- Reactionary tactics:

  - Attacking

  - Ambushing

  - Monopolizing

  - Avoiding

Problems of Perception (Cont.)

- Self-interested listening:
  - Selective listening
  - Literal listening
  - Filling in the gaps
  - Assimilating into prior understanding
- Giving advice.
- Offering support instead of listening.

Asking Questions

- Purposes:
  - Reducing uncertainty
  - Connecting and finding mutuality
  - Checking perceptions
  - Overcoming the problems of perception and misunderstanding

Features of Questions

- Two types are open- and closed-ended.

- Open-ended questions help the other to learn, express, and evaluate.

- Empathic questions show concern.

- Questions check inferences.

Features of Questions (Cont.)

- Probes help the other express his deeper concerns, solve problems, gain perspective.

- Patiently wait for answers.

- Avoid using argumentative questions.

- Avoid putting down the other's answers.

- Appreciation of answers is crucial.

1.19

Ways to Improve Memory

- Use association.

- Identify and isolate messages.

- Generate priorities.

- Create a structure.

- Use repetition and rehearsal.

1.20

Eight Ways of Responding

1. Passivity
2. Paraphrasing
3. Questions
4. Support
5. Advice
6. Feedback
7. Assessment
8. Confrontation

1.21

Giving Advice

- Upside:
  - Giving advice can provide people with a path forward.
  - Giving advice that people want and can use benefits them.
- Downside:
  - Giving advice prematurely might alienate the recipients.
  - Giving unsolicited advice wastes everyone's time.

1.22

Giving Advice (Cont.)

- Guidelines:

  - Make sure you are giving advice in order to benefit others, not yourself.

  - Wait until you understand those involved and the situation.

  - Wait for a teachable moment.

  - Wait until they ask for it.

  - Use their aspirations and help them accomplish their goals.

  - Give advice about one step they can take.

Defensive Behaviors

- Evaluation of others or their ideas
- Attempt to control the conversation or situation
- Use of strategy or concealed motivations
- Neutrality and noninvolvement
- Certainty or dogmatism

1.24

Supportive Behaviors

- Nonjudgmental description

- A problem orientation that is not imposing

- Spontaneity or noncalculating behavior

- Empathy with the speaker

- Equality based on mutual trust and respect

1.25

Guidelines for Feedback

Effective

- Choose good timing or ask, "Is this a good time?"

- Be descriptive: "You just said that you do not care."

- Focus on things the person can change.

Ineffective

- Disregard timing and person is unreceptive.

- Be evaluative: "You are an uncaring person."

- Focus on things the person cannot change.

1.26

Guidelines for Feedback (Cont.)

Effective

- Be direct.

- Be simple.
- Be brief.

Ineffective

- Be passive-aggressive or irate about something else.

- Be abstract and complex.
- Be long-winded.

1.27

The Powerful Listening Model Recapped

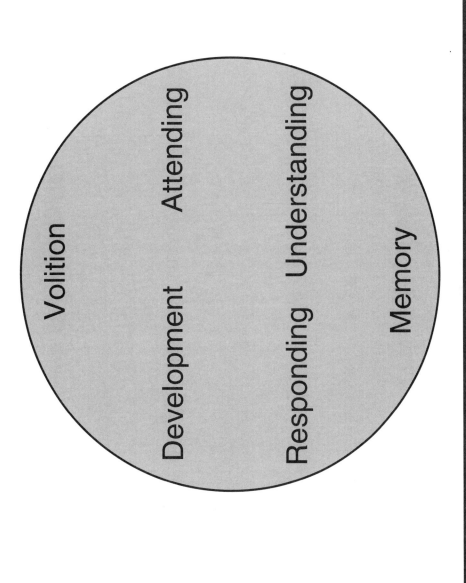

Volition
Attending
Development
Responding
Understanding
Memory

1.28

Steps in the Development Process

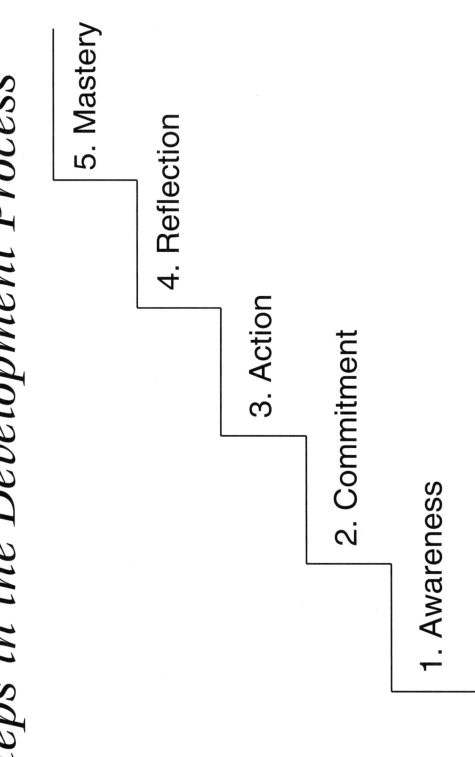

5. Mastery

4. Reflection

3. Action

2. Commitment

1. Awareness

1.29

Assertiveness

Powerful skills for assertiveness, authenticity, and advocacy

2.1

Module Agenda

- Total time: Four hours

- Introduction

- Relationships

- Assertiveness

- Appreciation

- Asking

2.2

Module Agenda (Cont.)

- Break: Fifteen minutes

- Self-confidence

- The PRES model of advocacy

- Summary

2.3

Module Objectives

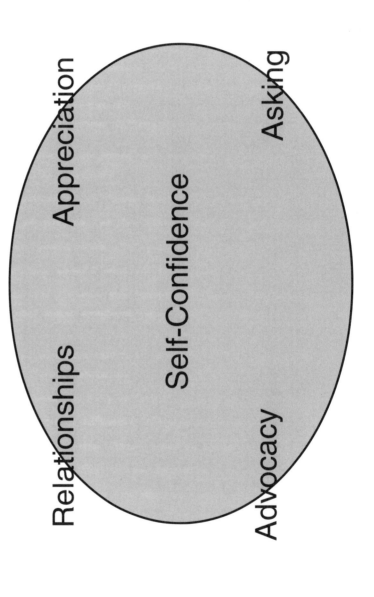

Appreciation

Asking

Relationships

Self-Confidence

Advocacy

2.4

Picture Game Rules

- Form into groups.

- Select team names.

- Decide who draws first.

- Win points by guessing the drawing.

- The team with the most points wins a prize.

Principles of Communication

1. Communication is two-way, not one-way.

2. All messages have content and relationship dimensions.

3. Relationships are either symmetrical or complementary.

2.6

Principles of Communication (Cont.)

4. You cannot *not* communicate

5. You cannot uncommunicate.

2.7

Content and Relationship Dimensions

Principle 2

Each message has two dimensions:

- Content—literal, or verbal

- Relationship—implicit, or nonverbal

Assertiveness, Passivity, and Aggressiveness

- *Assertiveness* is speaking up for your own rights and interests without violating the rights and interests of others.

- *Passivity* is not speaking up for your own rights and interests.

- *Aggressiveness* is acting for your own rights and interests in a way that violates the rights and interests of others.

2.9

Effectiveness and Assertiveness

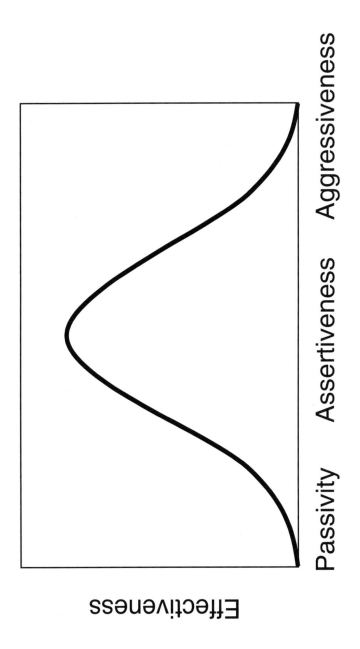

Effectiveness

Passivity   Assertiveness   Aggressiveness

2.10

Rules for the Slippery Egg Relay

- Each team has two spoons—one for the runner and the other for the next runner.

- Each team member runs the entire course with an egg on a spoon.

- Only the spoon can touch the egg. If anything else touches the egg, you must start over.

Rules for the Slippery Egg Relay (Cont.)

- The egg must stay on the spoon.

- When team members complete the course, they must transfer the egg using only the spoons. No hands!

- You must cheer your teammates.

- The first team to have all members finish and sit down wins!

Asking Quotes

- You miss 100 percent of the shots you do not take.

    —Wayne Gretsky

- If you don't ask, you don't get.

    —Mohandas Gandhi

- Never, never, never, never give up.

    —Winston Churchill

2.13

Asking Quotes (Cont.)

- We tend to get what we expect.

  —Norman Vincent Peale

- You must do the thing you think you cannot do.

  —Eleanor Roosevelt

Assertiveness Quotes

- Feel the fear and do it anyway.

  —Susan Jeffers

- All things are difficult before they are easy.

  —Thomas Fuller

2.15

Assertiveness Quotes (Cont.)

- Most of the important things in the world have been accomplished by people who have kept on trying when there seemed to be no hope at all.

  —Dale Carnegie

Assertiveness Quotes (Cont.)

- All that is necessary to break the spell of inertia and frustration is this: Act as if it were impossible to fail. That is the talisman, the formula, the command of right-about-face which turns us from failure towards success.

  —Dorothea Brande

Powerful and Powerless Speech

Powerful

- No qualifiers—"All men are created equal."

- No verbal pauses

Powerless

- Qualifiers—"I think that all men are created equal."

- Verbal pauses—"ah, er, um, uh, and . . . ."

2.18

Powerful and Powerless Speech (Cont.)

Powerful

- Declarative language—
  "When profits rise . . . "

- Positive attitude—
  "I will be happy to."

Powerless

- Hedges—"Don't get me
  wrong but . . . ."

- Negative attitude—"Only
  if I have to . . . ."

Intervening in Conversations

- Intervene when the listener:

  - Does not listen

  - Cuts you off

  - Is disrespectful

- Step 1. Decide whether to intervene.

  - Is the relationship important?

  - Does the behavior affect something important to you, a priority?

Intervening in Conversations (Cont.)

- Step 2. Give feedback.

  - State what was publicly observable about the person's behavior.

    - For example, "Just a moment, you began speaking before I finished my sentence."

  - Avoid being judgmental.

- Step 3. Ask for what you want.

  - "Please listen while I finish."

2.21

Nonverbal Assertiveness

- Appearance
- Space
- Voice
- Environment
- Facial expressions
- Posture
- Time

Nonverbal Assertiveness (Cont.)

- Movement:
  - Walk with an even stride.
  - Swing arms a little.
  - Keep head up.
  - Take in surroundings.
  - Glance carefully at others.
  - Walk briskly.

The PRES Advocacy Model

- *Point*
  - The proposed flextime system will serve the best interests of the organization.

- *Reason*
  - According to our HR analysis, we need to attract and attain the most talented people, and we need high morale in the face of our challenges.
  - The flextime system will be a lure to attract talent, and it will be a benefit to keep and motivate the talent we have, all without adding cost.

The PRES Advocacy Model (Cont.)

- *Example*
  - Two other business units in our company added flextime systems, and their attrition rates fell significantly.

- *Summary*
  - The best decision is to adopt the flextime system.

2.25

Steps in the Development Process

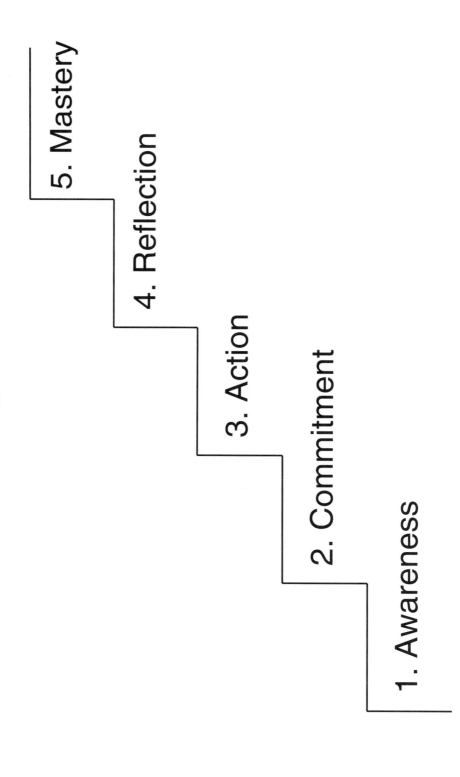

5. Mastery

4. Reflection

3. Action

2. Commitment

1. Awareness

2.26

Conflict Management

Powerful skills for productive conflict management and resolution

3.1

Conflict Archetypes

- Warrior
  - Is impeccable, competent.
  - Confronts and empathizes.

- Saint
  - Offers forgiveness, change of perspective.
  - Alters self and relationships.

Conflict Archetypes (Cont.)

- Teacher
  - Reframes.
  - Helps others develop, including opponents.

- Student
  - Seeks continuous self-development.

3.3

Module Agenda

- Total time: Four hours
- Conflict styles and strategies
- Integrative conflict management
- Negotiation planning
- Communication skills and cases

Module Agenda (Cont.)

- Break: Fifteen Minutes

- Communication skills and cases (continued)

- Third-party intervention

- Development in conflict management

3.5

Module Objectives

Conflict style and strategy

Negotiation preparation

Conflict management

Third-party intervention

Communication skills

3.6

Conflict Defined

- Conflict occurs when interdependent people pursue goals or values and perceive interference from one another.

3.7

Conflict Defined (Cont.)

- Key concepts:
  - Interdependence
  - Goals or values
  - Perception
  - Interference

Conflict Management Styles Grid

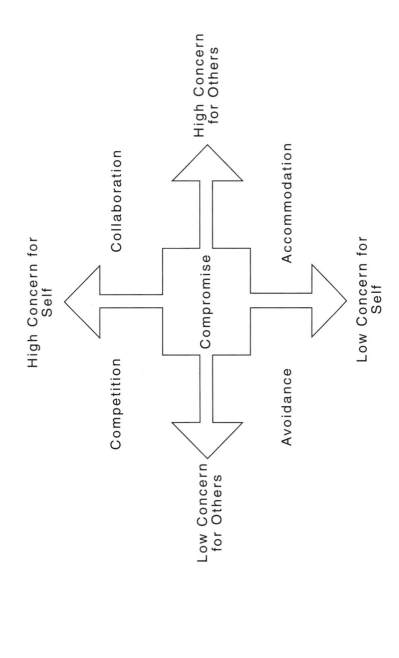

High Concern for Self

High Concern for Others

Collaboration

Competition

Compromise

Accommodation

Low Concern for Others

Avoidance

Low Concern for Self

3.9

Source: Adapted from R. Kilman and K. Thomas. "Interpersonal Conflict-Handling Behaviors as a Reflection of Jungian Personality Dimensions," Psychological Reports Vol 37, 1975 pp. 971–980.

© 2001 Joshua D. Guilar

Disbributive versus Integrative Conflict Management

Distributive

Win-lose

Competition =
Zero-sum game
+ 1 − 1 = 0

Compromise =
$+ \frac{1}{2} - \frac{1}{2} + \frac{1}{2} - \frac{1}{2} = 0$

Integrative

Win-win

Collaboration =
Nonzero-sum game
+1 + 1 = 2

Distributive versus Integrative Conflict Management (Cont.)

Distributive

Trade-offs, fixed-sum issues, and limited resources

Withholding information, deception, seeking information

Integrative

Creative solutions, overlapping interests, and variable-sum issues

Open communication, information sharing, shared inquiry

© 2001 Joshua D. Guilar

3.11

Negotiation Preparation Worksheet I

Your interests:
Their interests:
Creative options:
Your best option other than negotiating:
The least you will live with:

3.12

Negotiation Preparation Worksheet II

Your interests:	• Improve product quality. • Increase availability. • Maintain effective partnerships. • Keep costs as low as possible.
Their interests:	• Increase profitability. • Maintain the partnership. • Expand production capacity. • Improve product quality.
Creative options:	
Your best option other than negotiating:	
The least you will live with:	

3.13

Negotiation Preparation Worksheet III

Your interests:	• Improve product quality. • Increase availability. • Maintain effective partnerships. • Keep costs as low as possible.
Their interests:	• Increase profitability. • Maintain the partnership. • Expand production capacity. • Improve product quality.

Creative options:
- Help partner increase productive capacity by offering a new contract that will enable them to find financing for new equipment.
- New equipment will increase their productivity and profits and improve availability and quality.
- Form a joint task force to work on quality issues.

Your best option other than negotiating:
- Find a new partner.
- Manufacture the parts in-house.

The least you will live with:	• Increased availability • Increased quality • Minimal increase in costs

3.14

Communication Skills

- What to do before the conversation
- Conversational skills and insights:
  - Making "I statements"
  - Confirming the other person's point of view
  - Responding to attacks
  - Dealing with fallacies
  - Third-party intervention

What to Do before the Conversation

- Cool off.

- Find a convenient time.

- Prepare.

- Set the tone for a constructive purpose.

- Review supportive and defensive climates and communication skills.

3.16

I Statements

Example: I feel frustrated with the lack of progress on this project. I get worried when I see that four of your assignments are overdue. I am interested in determining commitments to action assignments today because I want us to complete this project on time and according to plan.

3.17

I Statements (Cont.)

- Four-step format

- Ownership—"I feel frustrated with the lack of progress on this project."

- Problem—"I get worried when I see that four of your assignments are overdue."

- Intermediate goal—"I am interested in determining commitments to action assignments today."

- End goal—"because I want us to complete this project on time and according to plan."

I Statements (Cont.)

Example language for the four steps

"I feel . . . when I . . . I would like you to . . . because . . ."

"I think . . . when you . . . I need . . . the goal . . ."

"I believe . . . when the . . . I want . . . our interests . . ."

"I don't like . . . to be the . . . I wish . . . so I can . . ."

3.19

Confirming the Other Person's Point of View

- Slow down the process.

- Shift to the other person's point of view.

- Imagine what the other person thinks and feels.

- Ask a constructive question.

- Confirm the person's experience.

- Offer to help as appropriate.

- Continue to negotiate.

3.20

Responding to an Attack

- Take time out.

- Take a deep breath, and be confident.

- Be silent for a while.

- Reframe the conversation.

3.21

Dealing with Fallacies

- Recognize the fallacy for what it is.
- Question its logic and data.
- Reframe based on valid logic and data.

Negotiation Process

- Form back into negotiation teams.

- Review preparation: five minutes.

- Meet with alliance partners in the other organization.

- Negotiate an agreement, or not: fifteen minutes.

- Record your agreement.

- Debrief and evaluate your negotiation process.

3.23

Third-Party Intervention

Topic

- Conflict styles

- Preparation

Relevance

- Assertiveness
- Integrative conflict management
- Collaboration

- Know interests of both parties.
- Prepare creative solutions.

Third-Party Intervention (Cont.)

Topic

- Responding to attacks

- Responding to fallacies

- Reducing defensiveness

Relevance

- Cool off and respond; do not react.

- Set standards for valid information and decisions.

- Use open communication and shared inquiry.

Agreements

Collaborative climate
Listening for understanding
Shared information
Confirming their point of view

Focus on interest and creative solutions

Valid information and decisions
Objectively verifiable data
Reason—conclusions based on evidence and logic
Inferences and opinions when presented as such

Rules for the Conflict Game of Peril

- The objective is to score the most points.

- You score points as a team.

- You can confer with your team members, and you can make a move independently as well.

- Use your voice as a buzzer to signal that you want to make a guess—make a sound like "bagh."

- Pick a category and then a question for ten, twenty, thirty, or forty points.

3.27

Rules for the Conflict Game of Peril (Cont.)

- The group that answers correctly gets the points and makes the next selection.

- Any person can buzz and answer the question, but only after the question is read completely.

- No points are lost for a wrong guess, but the team must wait to go again until all other teams have had a turn.

Categories in The Conflict Game of Peril

Conflict styles and archetypes	10	20	30	40
Integrative conflict management	10	20	30	40
Negotiation preparation	10	20	30	40
Communica-tion skills	10	20	30	40

Module Agenda

- Total time: Four hours

- Conflict styles and strategies

- Integrative conflict management

- Negotiation planning

- Communication skills and cases

3.30

Module Agenda (Cont.)

- Break: Fifteen Minutes
- Communication skills and cases (continued)
- Third-party intervention
- Development in conflict management

3.31

Conversations for Coordinating Action

Powerful skills for aligning commitment and accomplishing extraordinary results

4.1

Three Questions

- What do you plan to contribute in this workshop today?

- How accountable are you for your experience in this group today?

- How much responsibility do you plan to take for the experience of others in this group?

Module Agenda

- Total time: Four hours

- Introduction

- Personal commitments

- Conversations for action

- Conversations for relationship and connection

- Conversations for cocreation

- Break: Fifteen minutes

4.3

Module Agenda (Cont.)

- Conversations for partnership and alignment
- Conversations for action and accountability
- Conversations for learning and completion
- Personal development plan
- Workshop conclusion

4.4

Module Objectives

Cocreation

Relationship and
connection

Partnership and
alignment

Learning and
completion

Action and
accountability

4.5

Your History of Commitments

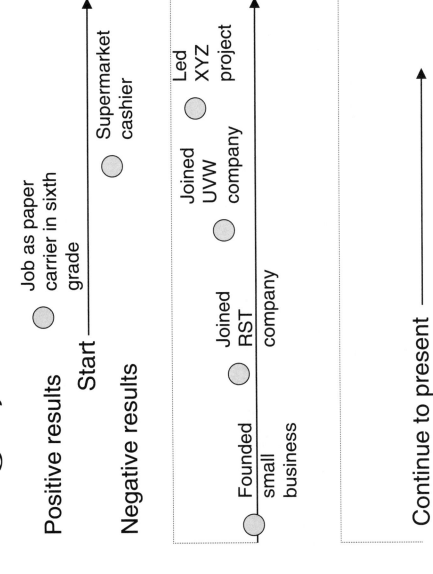

Positive results

Job as paper carrier in sixth grade

Supermarket cashier

Start

Negative results

Joined RST company

Joined UVW company

Led XYZ project

Founded small business

Continue to present

4.6

Projects and Commitments

- To undertake a project, as the word's derivation indicates, means to cast an idea out ahead of oneself so that it gains autonomy and is fulfilled not only by the efforts of its originator but, indeed, independently of him as well.

  —Czelaw Milosz

What Is It Time For?

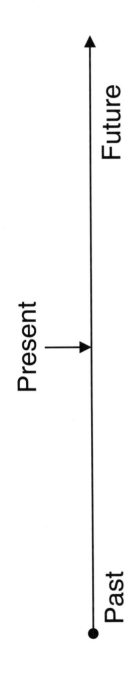

Past

Present

Future

4.8

Five Conversations for Coordinating Action

1. Relationship and connection

2. Cocreation

3. Partnership

4. Action and accountability

5. Learning and completion

4.9

Conversations for Connection

Connection	vs.	Disconnection
• Listening for mutuality		• Not listening, self-interested
• Authenticity and trust		• Superficiality and distrust
• Emotional intelligence		• Defensiveness
• Seeing each person as unique		• Stereotyping

4.10

Listening For . . .

- Commitments of others
- Opportunities for sincere appreciation
- Mutual interests
- Their concerns
- The listening of others

4.11

Authenticity

- Is saying tactfully what you are experiencing.

- Reveals others' and your assumptions.

- Brings resistance to light and provides for breakthroughs.

4.12

Authenticity (Cont.)

- Provides greater functionality.

- Is the antidote to being manipulative.

- Builds trust and relationships.

- Is the essential courage.

Emotional Intelligence

- Requires being aware of emotion as it happens in oneself, others, and the environment.

- Involves appreciation of oneself and others.

- Results in self-confidence.

- Is grace under fire, harmony, and ease in interpersonal relationships.

- Is a quality of leadership and connection.

4.14

Seeing Each Person as Unique

Problem

- Think and deal on the basis of inferences.

- Stereotype based on cultural and social backgrounds.

- Use polarizing language.

Solution

- Think and deal on the basis of facts.

- See each person as unique.

- Use language accurately.

4.15

Interpersonal Creativity . . .

Conversations for Cocreation

- Generates something new and useful through conversations between people.

- Is something we all can experience.

- Requires openness, support, and playfulness.

4.16

Interpersonal Creativity (Cont.)

- Comes through using tools:
  - Unlearning
  - Asking "what if" questions
  - Using associations and metaphors
  - Inviting diversity
  - Learning from mistakes
- Is fulfilled when we take a new idea into action with others.

4.17

¿Fi Tahv

4.18

What If?

4.19

Living What If . . . .

Problem: Recently your section doubled in size to 500 people. However, your department, which is a support function, has stayed the same size. You are swamped.

Creative Solutions:

- Have a brainstorming session.

- Seize this opportunity to lead change.

4.20

Living What If (Cont.)

- Redesign the department.

- Ask for more employees.

- Design protocols to prioritize work.

- Outsource to venders.

- Move to the Virgin Islands.

Creativity Killers

Problem

- Dismisses as impossible, or already knows it will not work here; sees future as continuation of past.

- Has no time for creativity—just decision and evaluation.

Solution

- Explore the possibility by reframing conversation.

- Make time and ground rules for creativity in the conversation.

4.22

Creativity Killers (Cont.)

Problem

- Squelch creativity by offering neither support nor openness.

Solution

- Use humor and tell stories about the benefits of speculation.

4.23

Your Resource Network

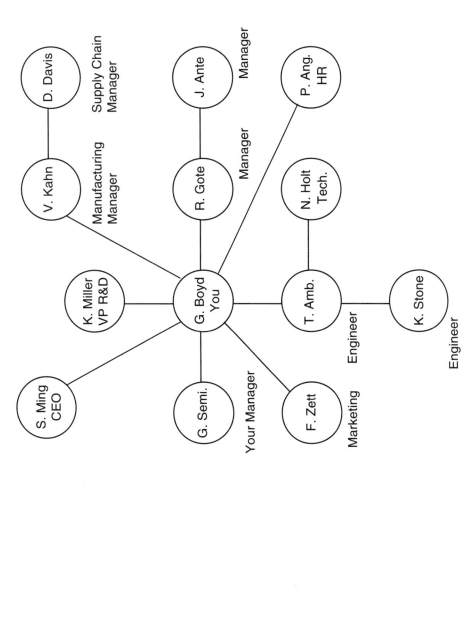

S. Ming
CEO

K. Miller
VP R&D

V. Kahn

D. Davis
Supply Chain
Manager

Manufacturing
Manager

G. Boyd
You

G. Semi.
Your Manager

R. Gote
Manager

J. Ante
Manager

F. Zett
Marketing

T. Amb.
Engineer

N. Holt
Tech.

P. Ang.
HR

K. Stone
Engineer

4.24

Interpersonal Partnership

- Occurs through conversation before taking action

- Determines the timeliness of actions, commitments, and projects

- Involves listening for commitments, politics, information, and resistance

- Encounters barriers—interpersonal, functional, and hierarchical

- Is based on cooperation, mutuality, and shared interests

4.25

Interpersonal Partnership (Cont.)

- Helps shape the project and its implementation.

- Involves trading on:

  - Your reputation for getting things done

  - Reciprocity—I help you; you help me

  - Alliances and connections

  - Position and assets

  - Diplomatic and interpersonal skills

4.26

Action and Accountability

- Requests that clarify:
  - *Who* is going to do
  - *What*, by
  - *When*, according to
  - *Which* conditions of satisfaction

4.27

Action and Responsibility (Cont.)

- Promises that hold:
  - Negotiated and voluntary participation
  - Internal commitment
  - Accountability
- Declarations that:
  - Identify breakdowns.
  - Clear away resistance and confusion.

Guidelines for Dialogue

- Suspend assumptions and certainties.

- Observe the observer.

- Listen to your listening.

- Slow down the inquiry.

- Befriend polarization.

4.29 Adapted from W. Issacs, "Taking Flight: Dialogue, Collective Thinking, and Organizational Learning," *Organizational Dynamics* 22, no. 2 (1993).

APPENDIX B

Workbook Activities

OVERCOMING OBSTACLES
TO UNDERSTANDING

Identify a conversation in which you felt defensive. This could be in your personal or professional life. Often, this occurs when you have a negative emotional history with someone. Somehow this person knew how to push your buttons.

Step 1. The Critical Incident

In the space below write a brief description of the last time you felt defensive in a conversation. Defensiveness is an emotional reaction where one feels attacked and vulnerable. This conversation could have occurred at work or in your social or personal life.

A critical incident where you felt attacked or vulnerable:

_____

_____

_____

_____

_____

_____

_____

_____

_____

_____

_____

Step 2. Your Experience

Analyze this experience. In the space below describe your experience on encountering this emotionally provocative conversation.

Your experience of the conversation—your emotional reaction:

_____

_____

_____

_____

_____

_____

_____

_____

_____

_____

Step 3. A More Effective Response

Next, consider how you could have behaved differently. In the space below, describe a more effective response.

How you could have handled this situation differently:

_____

_____

_____

_____

_____

_____

_____

_____

_____

EIGHT WAYS OF RESPONDING

Complete the sheet below for the conversation that you observe. Put a check in the appropriate box each time the listener-responder uses one of the ways of responding.

Listening Observation 1									
Passivity									
Paraphrasing									
Questions									
Support									
Advice									
Feedback									
Assessment									
Confrontation									

Listening Observation 2									
Passivity									
Paraphrasing									
Questions									
Support									
Advice									
Feedback									
Assessment									
Confrontation									

DEVELOPMENT PLAN FOR LISTENING

Reflect on the skills and attitudes you have studied in this workshop. Answer the question, What development area in listening would be a breakthrough for me? Work with the first step in the development process—awareness. Brainstorm answers in the space below. All possibilities are good possibilities.

Possible development areas:

_____

_____

_____

_____

_____

_____

_____

_____

_____

_____

_____

Next select an area for development. Consider the following criteria.

- The development goal would be a *breakthrough* for you in your relationships with others.

- The goal is *concrete*—you and others could observe whether you perform the behavior.

- The *results* of the goal are observable, too. If you integrate the behavior in your life, you can observe the positive effects on others and in your relationships.

- You select the goal freely and feel an *internal commitment* toward this goal.

Write your goal on the following form. Use more paper if needed.

Development Area 1

Your goal for development in listening:

_____

_____

_____

_____

Why you have selected this goal:

_____

_____

_____

_____

How you will accomplish this goal (include research, plans, behaviors):

_____

_____

_____

_____

Others who can help you accomplish this goal:

_____

_____

_____

_____

How you will follow up and know if you are successful:

_____

_____

_____

_____

Development Area 2

Your goal for development in listening:

_____

_____

_____

_____

Why you have selected this goal:

_____

_____

_____

_____

How you will accomplish this goal (include research, plans, behaviors):

_____

_____

_____

_____

Others who can help you accomplish this goal:

_____

_____

_____

_____

How you will follow up and know if you are successful:

_____

_____

_____

KNOWING WHAT YOU WANT

A key to effective assertiveness is knowing *when* to be assertive. Being assertive takes time and energy, and we need focus. One way to be effective is to prioritize. Why be assertive about things you do not care about? Save your assertiveness and focus it on things that are important to you. Know your interests.

Step 1. What You Want in Your Work and Professional Life

In the box below, write down the things that you want in your work and professional life.

What you want at work and professionally:

_____

_____

_____

_____

_____

_____

_____

_____

_____

_____

_____

_____

_____

_____

Step 2. What You Want in Your Personal Life

Next, make a list of things that you want in your personal, family, and social life. Brainstorm. These aspirations can be emotional, relational, material, or spiritual.

```
┌─────────────────────────────────────────────────────────────┐
│ What you want in your personal life:                          │
│                                                               │
│ _____   │
│                                                               │
│ _____   │
│                                                               │
│ _____   │
│                                                               │
│ _____   │
│                                                               │
│ _____   │
│                                                               │
│ _____   │
│                                                               │
│ _____   │
└─────────────────────────────────────────────────────────────┘
```

Remember what you want. Your priorities mark the important conversations where assertiveness belongs.

ASKING FOR WHAT YOU WANT

In this activity, you prepare to ask for what you want. Review the two lists you wrote in activity 2.1.

Step 1. Selecting

Select something you want to ask for from your professional or personal lists.

Something you would like to ask for:

_____

_____

_____

_____

_____

_____

Step 2. Why Asking Is Difficult

Next, consider the reasons why asking for this item (or receiving it) could be difficult. Write your reasons in the space below.

Reasons why asking for this item is difficult:

_____

_____

_____

_____

_____

_____

Step 3. Ask for It

In the box below record (1) what you will ask for, (2) who you will ask, and (3) how you will ask for it.

Remember these guidelines for asking:

- Be direct and specific.
- Ask with the expectation of success.
- Ask someone who has the power to give you what you want.
- Use humor.
- Ask a higher power.
- Ask with conviction and purpose.
- Ask again.

What you will ask for:

_____

_____

_____

_____

_____

Who you will ask:

_____

How you will ask for it:

_____

_____

_____

_____

_____

_____

_____

YOUR STRENGTHS AND ACCOMPLISHMENTS

Another tool for developing self-confidence is working with your strengths and accomplishments. Although we can shore up our weaknesses, this work is seldom as gratifying and productive as leading with our strengths.

Step 1. Your Accomplishments

In the space below, write down your major accomplishments.

Your accomplishments thus far in life:

_____

_____

_____

_____

_____

_____

_____

_____

_____

_____

_____

_____

_____

_____

_____

_____

_____

Step 2. What People Like about You

Next, write down what people like about you. Prod your memory for compliments. Believe them.

What others like about you:

_____

_____

_____

_____

_____

_____

_____

_____

_____

_____

_____

_____

_____

_____

_____

_____

_____

_____

_____

_____

_____

_____

Step 3. Your Strengths

Next list your strengths. Brainstorm a list of what you do well.

Your strengths:

_____

_____

_____

_____

_____

_____

_____

_____

_____

_____

_____

_____

_____

_____

_____

_____

_____

_____

_____

Remember your accomplishments, the compliments you've received, and your strengths. Build on them to accomplish even more.

TAKING A STAND

The purpose of this activity is to practice the skills for taking a stand on a controversial topic—a controversy either at work or in society.

Step 1. Brainstorm and Select a Controversy

In the space below, brainstorm ideas for a controversy you could discuss. Any idea is a good idea. After you make your list, circle one controversy you will address.

Controversies (brainstorm many, circle one):

Step 2. Use Powerful Language

In the next box, practice using powerful language for the controversy you wish to address. Using the guidelines for powerful speech, write a paragraph.

Write your argument using powerful language:

_____

_____

_____

_____

_____

_____

_____

_____

_____

_____

_____

_____

_____

_____

_____

_____

_____

_____

_____

_____

_____

_____

INTERVENING IN CONVERSATIONS

The purpose of this activity is to practice the three steps for intervening in a conversation. Read the following case. Then describe how you would respond.

You have decided to become more assertive. You feel that one person in particular, Terry, does not respect you in conversations. You have decided to intervene the next time he is disrespectful.

You and Terry are peers in a purchasing department, but he frequently makes "one-up" comments. You and Terry are in a room alone discussing a particular purchase. After you propose researching some alternate vendors for this purchase, Terry says seriously, "What do *you* know?"

In the space below, use the steps for intervening in conversations and describe how you would respond to Terry.

Your response:

PREPARING FOR ADVOCACY

In this activity, you will use the PRES advocacy model. First of all, determine an advocacy you wish to make. This issue can be anything at work, from a strategic direction for your company to a policy regarding the use of office supplies.

Step 1. State Your Point

Clearly make your point.

Point:

_____

_____

_____

_____

_____

_____

_____

_____

_____

_____

_____

_____

_____

_____

_____

Step 2. Give Your Reason

Provide the reason(s) you make this claim. Reason is evidence logically related to your point. Therefore, provide evidence and be logical.

Reason:

_____

_____

_____

_____

_____

_____

_____

_____

_____

_____

_____

Step 3. Give an Example

Where has this idea worked before? Give an example.

Example:

_____

_____

_____

_____

_____

_____

_____

_____

Step 4. Summarize

Finally, give a brief summary of your advocacy.

Summary:

_____

_____

_____

_____

_____

_____

_____

_____

_____

_____

_____

_____

_____

_____

_____

_____

_____

_____

_____

_____

_____

_____

DEVELOPMENT PLAN FOR ASSERTIVENESS

Reflect on the skills and attitudes you have studied in this session. Answer the question, What assertiveness skill or attitude would be a breakthrough for me? We are working with the first step in the development process—awareness. Brainstorm answers in the space below. All possibilities are good possibilities.

Possible development areas:

Next select an area for development. Consider the following criteria.

- The development goal should be a *breakthrough* for you in your relationships with others.
- The goal is *concrete*—that is, you and others can observe whether you perform the behavior.
- The *results* of the goal are observable. For example, if you perform the behavior well, you will observe its positive effects in others and in your relationships.
- You select the goal freely and feel an *internal commitment* toward this goal.

Write your goal on the following form.

Development Area 1

Your commitment to development in assertiveness:

_____

_____

_____

_____

_____

Why you have selected this goal:

_____

_____

_____

_____

_____

How you will accomplish this goal (include research, plans, behaviors):

_____

_____

_____

_____

_____

Others who can help you accomplish this goal:

_____

_____

_____

_____

_____

How you will follow up and know if you are successful:

_____

_____

_____

_____

_____

Development Area 2

Your commitment to development in assertiveness:

_____
_____
_____
_____
_____

Why you have selected this goal:

_____
_____
_____
_____
_____

How you will accomplish this goal (include research, plans, behaviors):

_____
_____
_____
_____
_____

Others who can help you accomplish this goal:

_____
_____
_____
_____

How you will follow up and know if you are successful:

_____
_____
_____
_____

NEGOTIATION PREPARATION

You will prepare for a negotiation. In this negotiation you will represent either GourmetPet.com or Beloved Incorporated. Read the case, and in the worksheet below plan your negotiation with your partner.

Your interests:

Their interests:

Creative options:

Your best option other than negotiating:

The least you will live with:

Case Study

Team 1. Owners of GourmetPet.com

You and your partner founded an e-business, GourmetPet.com, that retails gourmet food for pets. A large pet food company called Beloved Incorporated wants to buy your company.

You are interested in selling the company because you want the cash. However, you feel attached to the employees in the company and to the unique company culture. You want the forty-five employees to retain their jobs. Also, you both are willing to stay on in a general management position for three years, with average annual salaries of $350,000, to help with the transition. Given revenues and profit growth, you believe the company is worth $5 million. Company revenues were $4 million last year, and profits were 8 percent.

In early negotiations you and your partner have determined that Beloved wants to pay $3 million as up-front money for the purchase, although there are other avenues to provide payment over time. You also understand that Beloved would like you both to stay in management positions; however, they want an escape clause to terminate your positions if deemed necessary.

Case Study

Team 2. Chief Negotiators for Beloved Incorporated

You and your partners are Beloved Incorporated's chief negotiators in the company's bid to acquire GourmetPet.com. Your executive team sees the acquisition as a key strategy in taking market share in the new economy.

Due to a shortage of capital, you do not want to invest more than $3 million up front to acquire GourmetPet.com. You are, however, open to other means of payment over time.

You are aware that the owners of GourmetPet.com have created a unique corporate culture, and you are willing to let them remain in management positions with a contract for the next three years. You do want a cancellation clause, in the event that the current owners do not work out with Beloved Incorporated. You are willing to negotiate the conditions of this clause.

You want to acquire the company as soon as possible. Also, you want to keep the management salaries in line with Beloved's norms, which for such proposed positions would be less than $300,000 per year.

I STATEMENTS

In this activity you will design and communicate an I statement based on the following scenario.

You have a conflict with your manager, Jack. You have already negotiated with Jack for travel funds to visit a crucial customer in California. Earlier, Jack had agreed to your trip, and you told your customer to expect you. Now Jack has turned down your travel request and did not mention your earlier agreement. You have decided to confront Jack on this issue.

Write your I statement in the space below. Remember the formula:

1. Ownership—"I feel frustrated with the progress on this project."
2. Problem—"I get worried when I see that four of our assignments are overdue."
3. Intermediate goal—"I am interested in determining commitments to action assignments today."
4. End goal—"because we need to complete this project on time and according to plan."

I Statement:

CONFIRMING THE OTHER PERSON'S POINT OF VIEW

In workbook activity 3.2, you used an I statement to confront your manager, Jack. Unfortunately, in this next scenario, Jack responds defensively. After you pose your I statement, Jack retorts, "No, you cannot go to California, and that is that."

Remember the steps for confirming his point of view:

1. Take time to slow down the process. Take a breath.
2. Shift your thinking and feeling away from yourself and toward Jack's experience. Use your will power.
3. Imagine what he feels and thinks.
4. Ask a constructive question if you need information.
5. Confirm Jack's feelings, experience, and perspective. Act confidently as you do this for you are not surrendering your interests or your principles.
6. Offer to help Jack as appropriate.
7. Continue to negotiate.

Part 1. Information

In the space below, write what you would say for step 4 above.

Ask for more information:

_____

_____

_____

_____

_____

_____

_____

Part 2. Perspective and Help

Jack responds, "This is just a tough time for me right now. I do not have time to analyze your request. I'm sorry to say we might be over the budget this month. I do not know if we can afford this expense just now."

In the space below, write what you would say for steps 5 and 6. Remember you are not surrendering your interests or your principles.

Acknowledge perspective and offer help:

_____

_____

_____

_____

_____

_____

_____

_____

Now that you have confirmed and understood Jack's point of view, you are ready to continue the negotiation. Write how you would continue this negotiation in the space below.

Continue to negotiate:

_____

_____

_____

_____

_____

_____

_____

_____

_____

RESPONDING TO AN ATTACK

In this activity, you will respond to a verbal attack. Imagine this scenario.

You are an advertising consultant in a small advertising agency. Your manager has asked you and a fellow consultant, Chris, to direct a project. Unfortunately, you do not get along with Chris. You feel Chris blocks your ideas, tells you what to do, and is trying to control the project and make you his go-for who follows his instructions.

You decide to approach Chris, and he agrees to discuss your work relationship. You start by saying you want to collaborate and have an equal role with Chris. To that end, you need to establish standards for your work together.

Chris responds, "You have got to be kidding. I have worked here twice as long as you have, and I certainly do not intend to take orders from you."

Dialogue 1. Responding to an Attack

Remember the guidelines for dealing with an attack:

1. Take time out to make sure you act rather than react.
2. Try being silent for a while.
3. Reframe the conversation toward the interests that you both have at stake—in this case, the successful completion of the project.

In the space below, describe how you would respond to Chris. Follow the guidelines for responding to an attack.

Your response:

_____

_____

_____

_____

_____

_____

_____

_____

_____

_____

_____

_____

_____

_____

_____

_____

_____

_____

_____

_____

_____

This conversation continues in the next workbook activity on dealing with fallacies.

DEALING WITH FALLACIES

Chris responds to your intervention and appears to listen. He agrees to accommodate your interests, to collaborate with you, and to treat you as an equal.

Now you tackle the project itself to see how this new collaboration works. You meet with Chris again to make a decision on the storyboards for the advertising project. Both of you have been working on storyboards, and each of you brings an idea to the meeting. You take turns presenting your ideas.

After both presentations Chris says, "Your idea will never work. People just aren't attracted to this kind of thing." You disagree and believe your market research justifies your ideas.

In the space below, describe how you would respond to Chris. Remember the guidelines for dealing with fallacies:

1. Recognize the fallacy for what it is.
2. Question the logic and data.
3. Reframe the conversation based on valid logic and data.

Your response:

_____

_____

_____

_____

_____

_____

_____

_____

_____

_____

_____

THIRD-PARTY INTERVENTION

Role 1. Manager, or Third Party

You are the manager of a marketing department in a large division of a Fortune 50 company. Two of your people—David, who has worked for the department for fifteen years, and Cynthia, who has worked for the company for two years—are having a conflict. They have agreed to meet with you and discuss their work relationship. Your plan for the meeting follows:

1. Discuss the guidelines for integrative conflict management and secure each party's agreement.

2. Use these guidelines to facilitate their conversation.

3. State the objective: To improve understanding and the work relationship between David and Cynthia.

4. Have each party express their interests, or what they would like to ask of the other person (begin with Cynthia).

5. Give each person a chance to speak until understood by the other person.

6. Reach an agreement on how to manage or resolve the conflict.

7. Agree on a follow-up plan.

Role 2. David

You have agreed to play the role of David in an improvisational role-play. Read the following carefully. Try to make the points in the list below during the role-play conversation. In your role, respond positively to your manager's intervention and when your manager asks you to change.

General information. You have worked for the organization for fifteen years. You know the organization's culture and its processes, and you are deeply committed to the company's mission. You have a bachelor's degree in management.

Your feelings about Cynthia follow:

1. You believe she is very selfish.

2. You have heard that she treats others of lower status with disrespect. (You heard this secondhand from an administrative assistant).

3. She is pushing a project through the department that has not been discussed with the whole team. You want her to talk about the project with the team.

4. You do not trust her.

Role Play. Third-Party Intervention

Role 3. Cynthia

You have agreed to play the role of Cynthia in an improvisational role-play. Read the following carefully. Try to make the points in the list below during the role-play conversation. In your role, respond positively to your manager's intervention and when your manager asks you to change.

General information. You are new in the department. You have finished a master's degree in marketing, and you are eager to make your mark. The manager has asked you to design a marketing strategy for a new product. You are working hard to achieve excellence; however, you feel that some people in the department, particularly David, do not like you.

1. You would like David not to interrupt you when you speak at meetings.

2. You would like to have a supportive and collaborative work environment without the bad feelings you sense at present.

DEVELOPMENT PLAN FOR CONFLICT MANAGEMENT

Reflect on the skills you have studied in this session. Answer the question, What development in conflict management would be a breakthrough for me? You are working with the first step in the development process—awareness. Brainstorm and jot your answers in the space below. All possibilities are good possibilities.

Possible development areas:

_____

_____

_____

_____

_____

_____

_____

_____

_____

Next select an area for development. Consider the following criteria.

- The development goal would be a *breakthrough* for you in your relationships with others.

- The goal is *concrete*—that is, you and others could observe whether you perform the behavior.

- The *results* of the goal are observable. For example, if you perform the behavior well, you will observe its positive effects in others and in your relationships.

- You select the goal freely and feel an *internal commitment* toward this goal.

Write your goal on the following form.

Development Area 1

Your commitment to development in conflict management:

_____

_____

_____

_____

Why you have selected this goal:

_____

_____

_____

_____

How you will accomplish this goal (include research, plans, behaviors):

_____

_____

_____

_____

Others who can help you accomplish this goal:

_____

_____

_____

How you will follow up and know if you are successful:

_____

_____

_____

_____

Development Area 2

Your commitment to development in conflict management:

_____

_____

_____

_____

Why you have selected this goal:

_____

_____

_____

_____

How you will accomplish this goal (include research, plans, behaviors):

_____

_____

_____

_____

Others who can help you accomplish this goal:

_____

_____

_____

_____

How you will follow up and know if you are successful:

_____

_____

_____

_____

YOUR HISTORY OF COMMITMENTS

On the time line below, draw a circle and label the jobs, projects, and major commitments from your work life. Begin with the first job you can remember and proceed to your hopes for the future. If you found a job or project a positive emotional experience, place its circle above the line; if negative, draw it below.

Part 1. Time Line

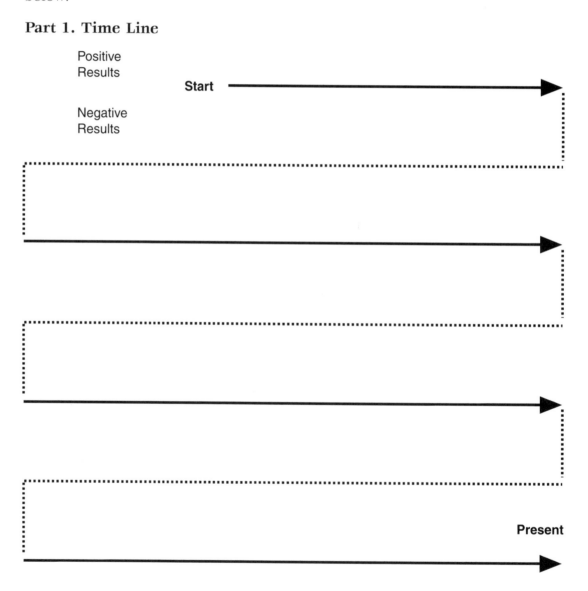

Part 2. Themes

Reflect on the trends and patterns you see on your time line. Then in the space below, write the themes you see in your history of work commitments. For example, what are your strengths? Focus on the items above the time line—that is, the projects and jobs you found emotionally positive.

Themes in your work history:

_____

_____

_____

_____

_____

_____

_____

_____

_____

_____

_____

_____

_____

_____

_____

_____

_____

_____

_____

_____

_____

YOUR WORK COMMITMENTS

Step 1. Your Current Commitments

In the space below, brainstorm a list of your current work commitments. You do not have to rank them.

Your present work commitments:

_____

_____

_____

_____

_____

_____

_____

Step 2. New Commitments

Make a list of the additional commitments you would like to make in the coming year.

Commitments you would like to make in the coming year:

_____

_____

_____

_____

_____

_____

_____

Step 3. What Is It Time For?

Finally, given your current commitments and the commitments you would like to make in the coming year, rank order your commitments in the box below. Rank your commitments by answering the question, What is it time for?

Your top work commitments in order of importance:

_____

_____

_____

_____

_____

_____

_____

_____

_____

_____

_____

_____

_____

_____

_____

_____

_____

_____

_____

Remember these commitments. We will return to them later.

RANKING YOUR COMMITMENTS

In the space below, write the highest-ranking work commitment from the last exercise.

Step 1. Your Top Work Commitment

Describe your top work commitment:

_____

_____

_____

_____

_____

Step 2. Those People Who Can Help You

In the space below, write the names of the people who can help you act on your commitment.

Names of partners:

_____

_____

_____

_____

_____

_____

_____

_____

_____

_____

YOUR NETWORK OF PARTNERS

Diagram below your network of partners. Use the list you made in workbook activity 4.3. The instructor will show you an example on an overhead.

Your Resource Network

PERSONAL DEVELOPMENT PLAN

Step 1. Reflection

Revisit the commitments you worked on earlier. Take some time to read and reflect on workbook activities 4.1 through 4.3, which outline your current, future, and prioritized commitments.

Step 2. Mission

Write your professional mission statement, declaring what you want to accomplish in your work. Usually a mission statement is brief. Examples of personal mission statements are:

- To innovate new uses for information technology that improve the effectiveness of people and organizations
- To help people develop in their work
- To help people through improving administrative processes in hospitals
- To create unique visual art characteristic of women's experience

My professional mission statement is:

_____

_____

_____

_____

_____

_____

_____

_____

_____

_____

_____

Step 3. Creative Tension

Write two brief essays. In the first essay, assess your current reality. Take a good look and answer the following questions: What is the reality of your behavior? Your connections and networks? Your performance? Are other members of your organization eager to have you as part of their team?

My current reality:

_____

_____

_____

_____

_____

_____

_____

_____

_____

_____

_____

_____

_____

_____

_____

_____

_____

_____

_____

_____

_____

Step 3. Creative Tension (Continued)

Now write a brief essay about the ideal future. Consider these questions: What kind of work relationships would you like to have? What results do you want? What connections and networks do you want? What communication skills would you like to master?

My ideal future:

_____

_____

_____

_____

_____

_____

_____

_____

_____

_____

_____

_____

_____

_____

_____

_____

_____

_____

_____

_____

_____

Step 4. Potential Areas for Development

Next select an area for development. Consider the following criteria.

- The development goal would be a *breakthrough* for you in your relationships with others.
- The goal is *concrete*—that is, you and others can observe whether you perform the behavior.
- The *results* of the goal are observable. For example, if you perform the behavior well, you will observe its positive effects in others and in your relationships.
- You select the goal freely and feel an *internal commitment* toward this goal.

In the space below, write your goal.

Brainstorm potential areas for development:

_____

_____

_____

_____

_____

_____

_____

_____

_____

_____

_____

_____

_____

_____

_____

_____

Step 5. Development Plan 1

Your commitment to development (identify concrete behaviors):

_____

_____

_____

_____

Why you have selected this goal:

_____

_____

_____

_____

How you will accomplish this goal (include research, plans, behaviors):

_____

_____

_____

_____

Others who can help you accomplish this goal:

_____

_____

_____

How you will follow up and know if you are successful:

_____

_____

_____

_____

Development Plan 2

Your commitment to development (identify concrete behaviors):

_____

_____

_____

_____

Why you have selected this goal:

_____

_____

_____

_____

How you will accomplish this goal (include research, plans, behaviors):

_____

_____

_____

_____

Others who can help you accomplish this goal:

_____

_____

_____

How you will follow up and know if you are successful:

_____

_____

_____

_____

Development Plan 3

Your commitment to development (identify concrete behaviors):

_____

_____

_____

_____

Why you have selected this goal:

_____

_____

_____

How you will accomplish this goal (include research, plans, behaviors):

_____

_____

_____

_____

Others who can help you accomplish this goal:

_____

_____

_____

How you will follow up and know if you are successful:

_____

_____

_____

_____

INDEX